Win the Battle of Your Mind

AF517221

Win the Battle of Your Mind

in the age of social media

REETA RAMAMURTHY GUPTA

EBD
EMBASSY BOOKS
www.embassybooks.in

Win the Battle of Your Mind © Reeta Ramamurthy Gupta, 2025

First Edition 2025,
Published in India by:
Embassy Book Distributors
120, Great Western Building, Maharashtra Chamber of
Commerce Lane, Fort, Mumbai 400 023, India
Tel: (+9122) -30967415, 22819546
Email: info@embassybooks.in
www.embassybooks.in

ISBN: 978-81-19726-61-5

Distribution Centres:
Mumbai, Ahmedabad, Bangalore, Kolkata, Chennai, Hyderabad,
New Delhi, Pune

All Rights reserved. No part of this publication may be reproduced, stored in a retrieval system, or transmitted in any form or by any means, electronic, mechanical, photocopying, recording or otherwise, without the prior written permission of the publisher.

Cover Design by Rishikumar Thakur for Embassy Book Distributors

Printed & bound in India by Parksons Graphics Pvt. Ltd.

Your income cannot exceed your personal development!

THE READING COACH:
A PERSONAL JOURNEY

Each one of us has that ONE question we'd rather not be asked.

For some it is "How many marks did you get?" For others it is "When are you going to have a baby?" or "When will you return my money?"

When I was growing up, the question I dreaded most was "What does your father do?" As questions go, this one is very basic and asked very routinely. My father was a loving man, rendered completely unstable by his mental condition; the fact that he was bipolar hit us many years after his death.

But when I was in school and in the throes of it, I had an identity crisis to deal with every single day. Therefore, very early in my life, I decided to build an identity for myself - that I was the most voracious reader you would ever meet - which rendered other personal questions redundant!

Nicknames such as *'scholly', 'chasmish*[1]*'* (I never had a number but wore spectacles to aid my identity), 'cher' (short for teacher), 'battery[2]' came my way, as I continued to wear the

1 Hindi slang for bespectacled.
2 Another slang for someone who wears spectacles.

proud badge of 'the girl who reads a lot'. I read voraciously, routinely got competitive even with my English teachers (thank God they continued to be kind!) and isolated myself from everyone else.

Not being invited to the 'cool' parties in school or even later in college, followed. This is exactly what I wanted; the fewer people I knew, the lesser I would be asked "What does your father do?" I read at least two books a week, from class fifth until my graduation. Yes, that's about a thousand books! Funnily enough, on his good days, it was my father who encouraged me the most.

The last stint of formal education came with my MBA. This was the first time I was away from home. Most of the batch lived away from their families; so personal questions were a rarity. I breathed a very marginal sigh of relief, while keeping 'the girl who reads a lot' alive.

One might say, I 'normalised' myself over two years, even as my identity carried me, albeit unconsciously. There was a cloudy consensus, that if I read a lot, I could write a lot too. So I was writer/editor of the management journal, writer/editor of the placement magazine, even writer of apology letters that other students wanted to write to the Dean in 'sincere language' that wasn't their own. I even wrote a letter from the Dean to a parent, reprimanding their ward!

I am proud to say my classmates were highly evolved and

focused on what we could learn from each other. They had all come to get the best job on campus (most of them at least). MBA was about who you were and who you were meant to become; not who your father was. I passed out with one of the best jobs on campus.

The 'girl who read a lot' lost her father the following year. The books though, remained.

It was several years later that I acquired this rather unique label called 'The Reading Coach'. Let me narrate a quick timeline.

My office has always been full of books and it has functioned as a pro bono lending library of sorts for passersby. *"Hey, do you have any tech biography?"* Or *"Is there a really thin self-help book you'd recommend,"* or *"My sister is pregnant and I want to give her a useful book to read,"* are common questions asked by friendly heads that pop in.

I took my love for books and reading a step further, in 2022, with my weekly book review column *BookStrapping*[3] on Network18. This was envisaged as a reader-friendly, pithy column that reviewed a contemporary classic every week. The trickle of conversations seeking book recommendations now became a stream. I started getting queries on my email and social media. One fine Sunday morning, I got an email from a parent about whether I would consider being a 'Reading Coach' to their child. Truth be told, I liked the title a lot. I told my children, *"Hey, guess what? Someone called me 'The*

3 Thank you Delshad Irani, the editor who supported this column from the word go!

Reading Coach'!" My daughter said, *"Sounds nice! It's true to who you are and has a nice ring to it."* My son, in contrast, was not that enthusiastic, *"As long as you don't show up in my college to do a session, I'm quite alright with it."*

As *BookStrapping* became more popular, a friend from B-School – a top notch HR professional – messaged me saying, *"I need to make people at my company read, Reeta. Can you do a programme for me?"*

This was music to my ears. Not only was I always happy to talk about books, but to talk about books and get paid for it was a dream come true. I had also lived and breathed tomes on the neuroscience behind the reading habit and was eager to talk about its benefits. So, I created a programme of my own and delivered it online with all the gusto I could muster. Little did I know that my session was being analysed in terms of metrics such as:

- How many people joined the session?

- Did people drop out midway?

But my most serendipitous moment was yet to come. The duration of the Q&A (post session) exceeded the time of the session itself. The questions kept coming!

Like Archimedes with the overflowing tub, I found my own Eureka moment as I navigated through these questions. I hadn't rehearsed for them, but somehow, the group and I

4 Thank you Maryanne Wolf and Stanislas Dehaene for all your work.

found answers together. Since that programme, I've been fortunate to be invited to conduct several sessions as 'The Reading Coach'.

At the end of each session, I've wanted to give away a book about the benefits of reading. A tribute to the work of the scientists and great minds all over the world that have made us understand and appreciate the neuroscience behind reading.

This is the one.

I would also like to dedicate this book to the work of P.N. Panicker, the father of India's Library Movement after whom we celebrate 19th June as National Reading Day.

TESTIMONIALS

"I found Reeta's scientific approach to the neuroscience and evolution of the reading habit accurate and creditworthy. Principally, there are four components of a scientific temperament – curiosity, open-mindedness, analytical mindset and humility. These are the root and soul of science. I found Reeta's work creditable on all four counts. She is devoted to reviving the reading habit and we must help her take this programme to as many people as possible."

– **Dr. Rajendra Jagdale,** *Director General and CEO at Science and Technology Park, an institute promoted by Department of Science and Technology, Government of India*

"This book aims to inculcate the reading habit – a habit that can potentially change the life of a person. The emotional satisfaction of reading a book and the self-sufficiency provided by it can be transformative."

– **Niranjan Hiranandani,** *Managing Director of Hiranandani Group*

"The Reading Coach session is professional and thorough, discussing not only the myriad benefits of reading but also very effective and easy techniques on inculcating this transformative habit of reading at any age into our daily lives!"
– **Rati Godrej,** *doctor at Godrej Industries Limited*

"We do need to think about how to make people read all over again. I agree that this is possible and extremely beneficial. How do we build the reading habit in these digital times? I don't know the answer but that's why this book[5] is being written."
– **Ajai Chowdhury,** *co-founder HCL*

"The why of reading is rather straightforward; our parents had 35-year careers, we have 45-year careers and our kids will have 55-year careers. Therefore, just the initial 15–17 years of learning is not enough. We have to create a personal learning plan. We have to experience **cognitive diversity** in learning to keep up."
– **Manish Sabharwal,** *co-founder Ashoka University and chief honcho of TeamLease*

"When you start working, you realise that information is power. At my peak – between the age of 30 and 40 – I would

5 Win the Battle of Your Mind

would read four to six hours a day! Literature was the first internet for me!"

– **Ramesh Damani,** *veteran investor*

"Reading is an underrated and under-utilised skill. The habit of reading has multiple benefits and the best part is that you can start at any age and time. As part of the Infosys Springboard, Pragati: Path to Future, a women's skilling initiative, we have been engaging with Reading Coach to ensure all the women learners pick up this habit and experience the multitude benefits in all walks of their lives and that of their families too."

– **Padma Bhamidipati,** *Associate Vice President - Learning | Driving Learning Engagement at Infosys*

"Reeta Ramamurthy Gupta's sessions as The Reading Coach are a classic example of simplified neuroscience. Her vast knowledge of books and immersion in reading keep audiences hooked from the beginning to the end. That is why we have done several seasons with her and every time she has something new to offer. We are sure her book will be the perfect mix of being light-hearted and informative, just like her sessions."

– **The Library team,** *HDFC Bank*

For the purpose of this book, whenever I use the word reading or reader, I am talking about **long-form reading** by choice. This could be a physical book or any form of ebook. If you're listening to an audio book, that's wonderful too. I have used the word 'digital reading' to refer to browsing emails, articles, presentations etc. on the phone or laptop. Scrolling on your phone, is, well… just scrolling!

A NOTE TO MY READER

We have had a rich literary tradition. The first orally transmitted text is likely to have been the Rig Veda, though historians differ on its timing. Bal Gangadhar Tilak suggests that since the Rig Veda refers to a solar eclipse in 4000 BC, it was narrated prior to that, while noted historian Arthur Llewellyn Basham suggests that its composition was between 1500–1000 BC. The writing of it came much later. If so, Enuma Elish, the oral Babylonian story of creation of 2500 BC, predates it.

Some accounts suggest that the Etruscan Gold Book, dating to about 660 BC, is the world's oldest multi-page book. It is difficult to decide which was the oldest because much of ancient literature is lost. India's Harappan script had 270 characters. Archaeologists also found an inkpot in the ruins, but where is the Harappan literature? Supposedly, the first reference to the word 'reader' came in 2300 BC. The first recorded author – the high priestess Enheduanna[6] – used the word in her songs. Suitably ancient as this reference is, it is still a blip in our billion-year evolutionary timeline. Scientists have repeatedly said that the human brain was not[7]

6 Enheduanna was a high priestess of the Mesopotamian kingdom of Akkad and the daughter of its ruler Sargon (reigned c. 2334–2279 BC). She wrote numerous works of poetry as well as temple hymns and myths.

7 More in Section 3.

fundamentally created with the architecture to read. All the other basic faculties, hearing, smell, touch and taste, are well developed at birth or within a few days of it, while the full range of sight strengthens over time. None of these activities need to be taught.

However, this is not true for reading. Reading is an ability or a type of evolved sense that needs to be taught[8]. A few parts of the brain have to coordinate to make this happen. And despite so many other ways to consume information, reading books has its place right at the top of the learning chain, while being both cheap and accessible.

Why so? And how will this book help? Much of the academic research on reading itself has been drowned by other, more sensational news. So I want to share the important ones with you here, and relate it to our daily lives. The scientific principles I speak about in the following chapters are proven and universally applicable.

And as you implement them, you will discover what works for you and thrive! It's because our minds are forever battling between scrolling and reading. And you're going to win this battle, because I'm going to tell you how to scroll less, read

8 More about this in Chapter 17.

more.

Do visit www.thereadingcoach.net and feel free to write to me.

Reeta Ramamurthy Gupta

THE
READING
COACH

"We transgress not because we try to build the new, but because we do not allow ourselves to consider what it disrupts or diminishes."

- Sherry Turkle, *Alone Together*[9]

9 Sherry Turke's important book, *Alone Together: Why We Expect More from Technology and Less from Each Other* published by Basic Books in 2011 is about a world in which one kind of freedom is traded for another. It asks the question, at what cost do we welcome technological advances into our lives?

TABLE OF CONTENTS

ANNEXURES

SECTION 1

YOU'RE BETTER OFF KNOWING THIS!

MIND PUZZLE 1[10]

The_e w_s o_ce a f_ish_rm_n a_d h_s wif_ wh_ dr_n_ th_ms_l_es t_ d_ath

Can you read the above?

How about this?

__ke _ay __ile _he __n __ines

Which is more difficult? And why?

10 Answer at the end of the section.

"Twice in your life, you are approved of by everyone - when you learn how to walk and when you learn to read."
– Penelope Fitzgerald

CHAPTER 1 NO 'BOOK' FITS ALL!

This story is set in 1993 pre-Google, pre-scrolling days. Back then, we wasted time in other ways, such as binge-watching VHS tapes or some form of cable TV with limited channels. Playing video games – basic ones – hanging out with friends at some basic version of a shopping centre, arcade, or local park, aimless conversations, trying all the forbidden things… etc.

I had a classmate Arvind Kedia (name changed for my own safety!). After our 10th standard results were out, where I had topped the class as opposed to Arvind who had got 61%, I found him distributing *laddoos* in the school foyer!

I asked him what the occasion was! He answered, *"I've passed with first class; what more occasion do you need, chashmish!"*

I couldn't believe my ears. At my home, there was no celebration because I had missed 100% marks in maths narrowly!

Arvind never participated in sports. He wasn't into elocutions or debates or participation in science experiments. He slept through history and geography class. But I couldn't laugh at him, because there was one thing about Arvind. His 61% was thanks to a 100 in mathematics. Don't ask me what his other scores were!

Arvind was the classic backbencher genius. We all know someone like him! His interests were largely non-conformist but ask him anything about mathematics and he would make the rest of us puff and pant as he found the solution effortlessly. He practised a lot with very thick books that had out-of-syllabus problems! He also read books written by mathematical geniuses – *Principles of Mathematical Analysis* by Walter Rudin was his favourite book! But he would never read Shakespeare for instance.

In sharp contrast was another classmate Riya. She had also scraped a 61%, but her score was an average of 50s and 70s. There was no subject where her expertise stood out! Once a year, Riya would emerge from slumber thanks to her bossy mom! The school would conduct a charity exhibition with stalls of merchandise sold by students. Riya's mother would miraculously appear out of nowhere to lead this. They sold merchandise like diyas, buntings[11], etc; all advertised as made by Riya, but actually made by her domestic help! Riya seemed disinterested in everything; once we were partners on a school project and Riya allowed me to do everything without having a single opinion or contribution. The girl confounded me!

Riya's zero-interest, zero-effort attitude to life is entirely different from Arvind's passion for mathematics to the exclusion of all else. Riya read nothing, Arvind read books about mathematics.

Now each of us needs to have **one talent that we can barter**

11 Torans

for a livelihood. (In case you are wondering, scrolling is not a talent!)

In the above example, one can assume that all other factors remaining unchanged, Arvind will have no problem making a living, while Riya might have to do things she doesn't like, till she actually discovers her passion and pursues it.

Careers and jobs are about earning a living by the work we do, which stems from a talent/skill we possess, a part of which we acquire by reading. The history of human progress is thanks to our ability to share knowledge with each other, which came about thanks to the evolution of writing and reading 5000 years ago!

Which brings us to a very interesting point!

It is now established without doubt that human beings taught themselves to read as a species.

As we read and apply what we read, we gain knowledge. This is an excellent time to consider the three questions that Socrates[12] posed about knowledge:

a. What do you know?

b. How do you know what you know?

c. Why should you care about it?

12 Most of my evolved readers will see the irony in quoting Socrates in a book on reading. Socrates believed in the power of oral transmission over writing and reading! In fact, the Socratic method is a form of argumentative dialogue between individuals, based on asking and answering questions, because he believed that writing was not an effective means of communicating knowledge.

CHAPTER 2 HOW DO YOU KNOW WHAT YOU KNOW?

This is a good question. And the correct answer would be 'many sources', one of which is books.

Going back to Socrates, the one who asked the question – he believed that face-to-face communication was the only way one person could transmit knowledge to another. Well, Socrates died in 399 BC. Almost 2400 years ago. There was no way he could have known about Google!

He lived in an entirely different time and we can safely give him the benefit of the doubt and accept that oral communication and debate will always have its merits; more so in a **one-to-one world.**

But as the population of the world expanded and the world became **one-to-many,** it was important for learned folk to write and transmit information. There are several key inventions[13] that significantly changed how we communicated over time, starting with the alphabet systems almost 4000 years ago. Thanks to the invention of paper by Ts'ai Lun and then the printing press by Gutenberg, writing and reading became part of our lives. Thus, the massification of knowledge by reading and writing happened about 500 years ago. Interestingly, this

13 Annexure 3 talks about key inventions in communication, (big and small)

is also the period where we have seen much of the scientific progress we enjoy today.

Let's attempt to answer[14] the three questions posed by Socrates.

1. What do you know?

Can you answer this accurately at all? If you're a doctor, you know medicine and outside of this – based on your interests – you may know the rules of cricket or music or chess, and have the functional knowledge needed to perform life activities. Chances are, your medical degree involved a fair amount of reading and practicals, both.

2. How do you know what you know?

Formal education? Maybe your elders passed it on. Maybe you learnt by observing, imbibing or travel. Perhaps you heard a podcast or watched a video (again, not something Socrates would've thought of) or read a book. "Books are meme delivery vehicles," explains Sahil Vaidya, a young Forbes 30 under 30 advertising genius and founder of the agency 'The Minimalist'. This is provided you understand a meme as an idea that rips through the public consciousness! Books propose original ideas; such as *The Selfish Gene* by Richard Hawkins (where the word meme was first used, to sound like 'gene') or *The True Believer: Thoughts on the Nature of Mass Movements* by Eric Hoffer. Books follow the 'The Lindy Effect', which is a theory that the longer something has been around, the more likely it is to continue to exist. In other words, 'time' is the best proof of the value of a book. This is why podcasts and shows try to decode the ideas in books.

14 You can answer these questions in your own way too and send it to me via www.thereadingcoach.net

3. Why should you care about it?

What you know helps you earn a living and develop your own identity. So you can say, "I am a teacher, I am a software programmer, I am an artist." In the grand scheme of things, **'what you apply yourself to matters',** so you need to keep learning more by being an agile learner and applying it as you go along.

You will see for yourself that reading plays a major role in all the above answers; **however, reading will play a major role only if it is your decision to allow it.** It's your choice to read.

Interestingly, Stanford Professor Ed Batista says, *"It's important to make good decisions…so I spend much less time and energy worrying about making the right decision, and much more time and energy ensuring that any decision I make turns out right."*

The question of whether you decide to become a reader or not may NOT create two parallel universes – one in which you're happy and the other in which you suffer! However, if you decide to spend all your time scrolling headlines, tweets, or brief summaries, you know you cannot reclaim that time!

Here's a poem to explain my point:

I scroll, I scroll, through endless feeds,

Lost in a world of non-deeds.

A baby, a cat, a dance, a fleet,

I waste my time to the scrolling beat.

Oh, there's a headline, bright and bold,

But I'll skip the details, I'm too bored, but sold.

on 10-second clips, and useless facts,
By the time I blink, the damn thing redacts!
Where's my focus and mental flair,
Is this an attention nightmare?
The hours slip by, I don't even know,
Where did they go? Where did they go?
I know things I'll never need …
But learnt nothing from this mindless feed.
I've Googled celebrity hook-ups and their fights;
But have I wished mom goodnight?
My tasks, easily begun but never done!
Succumbing to the clock, waiting for none!
So here I am, lost in this maze
An absent-minded online daze.
No wisdom gained, just dopamine highs,
And yet, scroll – 'cause it feels so damn nice!

Relatable?

But what if you did commit to SOME KIND OF deep, immersive, consuming work. This will surely result in a parallel universe for you! One such resident of a parallel universe is Olympic swimmer Michael Phelps, who has spoken about the role of reading in his mental preparation for competitions. Phelps has read numerous books on sports psychology, visualisation, and goal-setting, which have helped him stay focused and motivated throughout his career. He not only invested in his core of swimming but also in understanding the psychological factors that influence performance and was able to dominate his sport!

Michael Phelps' example is important because reading is not the preserve of the nine-to-five office goer or the business owner alone. Swimmers, chess masters, rappers – everyone can benefit from reading. Ask actress Reese Witherspoon about the billion-dollar corporation[15] she created as an actor, thanks to her love of reading!

Anyone who puts in deep, immersive work lives in a parallel universe.

If you're not willing to put in the work, you won't get the visa to that universe! To quote Sahil Vaidya again, "People are great at speaking, not so much at writing. There is no permanence to audio waves, but the minute you ask someone to write something down, it is more permanent and challenging. Similarly, reading is also a more complex cognitive process than speaking." And we all know that the results of any action depend on the effort put in. So agreed!

15 Reese Witherspoon's company is Hello Sunshine, a media and production company that creates and promotes content by and about women and adapts books by women authors. In 2021, Hello Sunshine was sold to Candle Media, a media firm backed by the private equity group Blackstone Group, for $500 million.

CHAPTER 3 WHY SHOULD YOU CARE ABOUT WHAT YOU KNOW?

Ask yourself this question:

"Can I get by in life without understanding even one subject in detail?"

'Expertise' of some kind is critical for survival; knowledge economy or not. Expertise is a level beyond 'passable' subject knowledge. And this is where 'reading' comes in. There's some magical aspect to reading that we don't fully comprehend!

After all, our brain literally performed high-level calisthenics[16] to learn how to read. Why would the brain make this much effort? At some point, our survival as a species depended on it. Reading has given us a lot to be grateful for:

- The ability to understand abstract concepts
- The ability to collaborate
- The ability to consider new perspectives

The list is long and is part of what we think we know. All of us MUST care about what we know. This is part of the reason I've written this book! Let me phrase my motives as questions here.

1. Do you get influenced easily? Does this help you?

"A vast majority of us, when confronted with difficult choices or

16 More about this in section 5

controversial subjects, are holding on to whatever explanations are readily available, making us more susceptible to biased opinion and poor information. We don't form our opinion based on any study of our own. Instead, we align with whatever is most convenient at the time."

Terrible isn't it? Smita is a tall, exceptionally pretty girl. Every morning, as she makes her way to office, everyone from the guards at the gate, to those who verify her access card, to the peons in her own office, await her entry. After all, she's rather lovely! Smita is confident about her appearance and makes the effort to enhance it with her grooming and her 'ramp walk' to office every morning is nothing short of a little celebration of our universal admiration of beauty. So far, so good!

Imagine my curiosity when, the other day, I saw Smita crying in the afternoon. Her boss, a brilliant businesswoman, had chided her about her performance. Smita said, "I am excited about walking into office every morning. I think I got carried away by the fanfare of it. I am not contributing at all, and every time I want to feel good, I walk to a new floor of the office building and soak in the admiring glances! But that's short-lived. I have to reconnect with my own purpose."

I couldn't help myself. I gave her my own copy of Brene Brown's *I Thought It Was Just Me But It Isn't,* and made her promise me that she would read it end to end. I knew she would find herself.

2. How do you determine your own value?

Smart folks have put measurement systems in place everywhere. 'You can only manage what you can measure' goes the common saying. Your value is closely associated, among other things, with:

- Your ability to influence people
- Your ability to get things done
- Your level of financial freedom.
- Your level of spiritual awakening.

It is important to focus on awakening your own creativity as the surest way to unlock your value in any of the above areas. Reading is a proven way to unlock personal creativity. In his letters to his brother Theo, Vincent Van Gogh documented what he called "a more or less irresistible passion for books." He spoke of authors Victor Hugo, Charles Dickens, Beecher Stowe and "other less classic authors" among his list of reads in 1880!

3. What is the cost of our continuously declining attention span?

Many of us today live in a constantly online world. Here, time flows swiftly. **What this means is that you can be 'watching something' for over six to eight hours and yet not really learn anything of value. You jump from reel to reel or website to website. In this 'continuous partial attention' cycle, information hits you but is largely not retained.** With every notification or jump, the dopamine release keeps us hooked, even as receiving a message other than the one we are waiting for leads to a letdown.

So, the question is: **did technology just replace other addictions like smoking, drugs and alcohol with smartphones and social media?** There are billions of dollars going into keeping us hooked! Reflect on the following:

- When we choose mindless browsing over a focused activity like reading or an intense physical workout, **it seems 'free'** but is going to **cost us in an expensive way!** Because nothing is free! There's a lot of research dollars going into tempting your mind to stay distracted and lure you into traps. Let me say this, **we cannot even begin to understand** the subtle power of lights, colours, suggestions, persuasions coming at us online.

- We live in constant 'task switching mode' – email to WhatsApp, WhatsApp to report, report to Instagram, Instagram to Zoom, Zoom to search bar, article to ad, ad to video, back to email – without any real need to jump around like this! This is causing cognitive confusion and disorder. This 'partial continuous attention[17]' is already reducing the quality of our output[18]. Except for the time when we sleep (which is also disturbed thanks to mindless OTT viewing just before bedtime), there seems to be no downtime for our brain faculties to rest.

A good follow-up question would be, is this taking good dollars away from things that are harder to do? Like building green technologies, better curricula in schools or doing research on less polluting industrial processes?

Okay, this just got a little heavy, but we can close with this. Ralph Waldo Emerson wrote in his brilliant essay 'Quotation and Originality', "If we encountered a man (person) of rare intellect, we should ask him (her) what books he (they) read.

17 Linda Stone coined the term Continuous Partial Attention in 1998 and it is defined as "the process of paying simultaneous attention to a number of courses of incoming information but at a superficial level." Stone herself has explained that this is different from what we call multitasking.
18 Check out the chapter on 'Full attention zone'

4. Are we choosing our leaders based on rational criterion?

Do you think the leaders of the world are making sensible decisions at all times? Invading other countries? Aiding and abetting terrorism?

The real dangers of 'monomaniacal, one-sided thinking' by people not open to diverse perspectives are already being felt by all of us. And reading is a good prescription to 'moderate' extremes of thought and behaviour by opening our minds to other points of view.

Franz Kafka famously said, *"I think we ought to read only books that bite and sting us. If the book we are reading doesn't shake us awake like a blow on the skull, why bother reading it in the first place?"*

Wouldn't it be fun to put some cognitive eligibility criteria before allowing people to stand for elections? Can we have a political prep program?

Dear candidate, if you want to join politics after five years, here's your reading list. Basis this, you have to pass an exam to get a ticket! Each book is entirely different from the other and you will definitely not agree with all the authors. But

still you have to study them for the exam!

Let's face it, we don't have much sway over (some of) them, once they get elected. In old times, leaders didn't even need to get elected. They just had to kill or threaten to kill more people than the boy next door! Remember Timur? (1370-1405). The ruler once ordered the construction of a tower made out of living men, one stacked on top of another and cemented together, in present-day Afghanistan. What one-on-one dialogue would Socrates have had with Timur? Quite the page turner that would be!

5. Who is going to solve the problems of the world?

Are we still talking about reading[19]? This has become really ponderous.

First up, can we candidly admit that we don't actually understand all the problems that the intellectuals of the world are talking about because we have not invested enough time to get familiar with the words or concepts they are referring to?

Blinded by convenience, we casually take sides about issues that matter, without actually applying ourselves. A trait fostered by social media.

The long-term thinking needed to solve the real problems of the world is going to come from deep work, clarity of thought, cohesion of actions and unity of purpose. This in turn requires tolerance of diversity, the willingness to develop consensus based on 'real' cognitive alignment and high-level cooperation.

19 Check chapter on readers will save the world.

Trigger-happy people with low attention spans cannot deliver the above. Myopic actions tend to ricochet as soon as they meet reality. Therefore, our education systems must encourage additional reading about varied points of view.

6. Are all readers intelligent?

I know many intelligent people who don't read. They just follow one or many of the other modes of learning we will discuss soon in the HELP matrix[20].

A major bias among readers is that they believe fiction to be "a waste of time!" I had a discussion on this with the very enterprising Ganeshprasad Sridharan of the Think School podcast, who said his reading philosophy was more about 'Just in Time' rather than 'Just in Case' and that he read only quality non-fiction to seek answers to his problems. I shared a lot of data with him about the benefits of fiction and he was broadminded enough to listen patiently. Unlike many people who credit their parents for being the trigger for their reading habit, Ganeshprasad says that when his mom gave him the book *Megaliving* to read in eighth grade, he wasn't ready. He rediscovered reading much later when he found a 'clear benefit' for it. He credits authors like Simon Sinek, Tony Fadell etc. for his love of reading.

In fact, during one of my sessions as The Reading Coach, I spoke about the benefits of reading fiction, only to have two girls come and hug me very tight! *"Thank you ma'am for talking about the benefits of reading fiction. Since we were kids, everyone around us is convinced we have wasted our whole lives*

20 Chapter 11

with our noses buried in stories."

Studies have found that reading fiction[21] tends to retrain the brain to stay open, comfortable with ambiguity, and able to sort through information more carefully.

Angus Fletcher[22], who combines neuroscience with literature to unlock what stories do to our brains, says,

"When your brain enters a story, it jumps out of your perspective into a character's perspective. That's some of the great fun of reading a book. When you make that jump, you shift out of your biases. You shift out of your own hopes and fears. You let go of the things that prevent you from opening your mind to other possibilities. And that naturally opens you up to being more imaginative, more creative."

Reading non-fiction on the other hand, enables us to derive explanations and reasons for what is happening around us, compare how similar things panned out in history, rather than just feeding on the opinion and propaganda we see on the 'news'.

The common link that imparts the above benefits is 'cognitive diversity' or exposure to a vast genre of authors. We will also get into the decagonal benefits of reading in a subsequent chapter.

21 Some kinds of dark fiction don't necessarily feature in this bracket.

22 Dr. Angus Fletcher studies literature's usefulness, treating it as a practical tool for alleviating poverty, hunger, heartbreak and other physical concerns by employing a range of empirical methods, from ancient rhetoric to modern science. His research has been funded by the National Science Foundation, the National Endowment for the Humanities, the Mellon Foundation and the Academy of Motion Picture Arts and Sciences. Fletcher has taught for University of Southern California, Stanford and Teach for America.

CHAPTER 4 BOOKS AND THE VALUE OF PERMANENT INFORMATION

This is going to blow your mind, dear habitual doomscrollers.

Keep the following in front of you: a book, a newspaper, an Instagram post and a pamphlet about a neighbourhood shopping sale. Then, read this.

In his book *Same as Ever: A Guide to What Never Changes,* author Morgan Housel[23] famously says,

There are two types of information: permanent and expiring. Permanent information is: "How do people behave when they encounter a risk they hadn't fathomed?" Expiring information is: "How much profit did Microsoft earn in the second quarter of 2005?" (Or which actor is having an affair with whom!)

Expiring knowledge catches more attention than it should, for two reasons.

- One, there's a lot of it, eager to keep our short attention spans occupied.

- Two, we chase it down, anxious to squeeze insight out of it before it loses relevance.

Come to think of it, we do get sucked into temporary

23 Morgan Housel is a partner at The Collaborative Fund and author of *The Psychology of Money.*

information! Whether it is which designer made the clothes for the Ambani wedding or the vagaries of Virat Kohli's batting form, we are all glued to our screens reading about it for five weeks or five minutes. On the corporate side are the quarterly results of listed companies, which are actually no more than a temporary performance card! They are not a big 'do or die' statement! Often, when a company is in the middle of a massive transformation, results tend to be dull in the short term to accommodate the long term! Much like Kohli's bat!

In Morgan Housel's words, *"Permanent information is harder to notice because it's buried in books rather than blasted in headlines."*

A deep study of spirituality or any such discipline would count as permanent knowledge. And given the **very nature of deep study,** the benefits are huge. **The characteristics of permanent information are that:**

- It answers the question 'how'. How to manage ambiguity, how to rise again after failure.
- It never expires, letting you accumulate it.
- It also compounds over time, leveraging off what you've already learnt.
- Permanent information helps us to build convictions of our own, so as not to get swayed easily.

On the other hand, expiring information tells you 'what' happened. It is almost the entire bulk of your social media feed! It is sensational and sucks you in and you could discuss it over a bar-hangout or lunch meeting and exchange a few laughs (even though social capital and engagement has its merits in the right doses).

Hence, it is important to distinguish between permanent and temporary information early in life and develop your base. To close this chapter, one may not be able to better the great Samuel Johnson's[24] observation:

"It is common to find young men, ardent and diligent in the pursuit of knowledge; but the progress of life very often produces laxity and indifference; and not only those who are at liberty to choose their business and amusements, but those likewise whose professions engage them in literary inquiries, pass the latter part of their time without improvement, and spend the day rather in any other entertainment than that which they might find among books."

In other words, Samuel Johnson wonders why those who 'know' that they need to invest in self-development will do anything BUT read! Reading 'quality books' is the most easily accessible and affordable way to access permanent information that compounds over time.

24 Samuel Johnson, often called Dr. Johnson, was an English writer who made lasting contributions as a poet, playwright, essayist, moralist, literary critic, sermonist, biographer, editor, and lexicographer.

EXPERT READER ESSAY - 1

LITERATURE WAS MY INTERNET

I always loved reading. I grew up in South Bombay and often my parents would send me on errands. The most common one was to get pao or bread. Those days, the pao would come wrapped in a random paper and I would even read that! This was when I was about 10 years old.

I was fortunate that my father was very fond of reading. This was the pre-internet era and my father had a subscription to the best newspapers and magazines of the time. From Time Magazine to Newsweek and The Economist, everything would come home and my father would be the first person to read them. Over time, we developed a healthy competition around who would get to reading what first! At the time, I would've been a 16-year-old at most.

I had developed a habit of keeping pace with what was happening across the world and this only compounded with age. When you start working, you realise that information is power. At my peak – between the age of 30 and 40 – I would read four to six hours a day! Literature was the first internet for me. I was in the investing business. In my profession the most important art and preparation is reading, as expressed lucidly by both Charlie Munger and Warren Buffet. Unlike a profession like engineering or hairdressing, the business that I am in involves developing broad thinking across subjects. We have to read a lot to make sense of the world around us and consider all factors before investing.

My family often calls me a book with two legs, which is what Munger was called. There was a time when my wife would pull my leg and say, "You are all reading and no acting." But that's the whole point of investments! This is a deep study and involves tremendous thinking, self-reflection and analysis; there is very little 'acting'. I imagine that some other professions would be like this too! I'd like to believe that she understood my point of view eventually! It is very difficult to please our wives! Ha ha!

Even though a majority of what I read earlier would be annual reports and balance sheets, I developed a love for non-fiction. The pile of newspapers too increased over time and in addition to our Indian newspapers, I have devoured editions of The Economist, Wall Street Journal, The Financial Times and New York Times over the years.

I also developed a keen interest in biographies. From Rockefeller *(Titan: The Life of John D. Rockefeller, Sr.)* to Andrew Carnegie's autobiography *(The Gospel of Wealth)*, I have read everything I could get my hands on. Two books I have enjoyed tremendously are Gandhiji's *My Experiments with Truth* and Charles Lindbergh's *The Spirit of St. Louis.* The latter is an autobiographical account about the events leading up to and including his 1927 solo trans-Atlantic flight and sparked my interest in travel.

Somehow, I never took a liking to fiction! Perhaps because I believe that real life is stranger than fiction.

Now that I am older, my eyes are weaker and I don't read for the six hours I used to! However, I still continue to read because it is my time of unalloyed pleasure. Reading consistently has also made me more spiritual. It's the one habit I have strived to inculcate in all, especially my own children and grandkids.

Essay by Ramesh Damani, *veteran investor.*

SECTION 2

READERS KEEPERS, SCROLLERS WEEPERS!

Check for solution to mind puzzle 1[25]

MIND PUZZLE 2

Read the sentence.

THE BINGULLY SHEP JUDED THE JINGULLY MEP

And answer the questions

1. How was the shep?
2. Who juded the jingully mep?
3. How was the mep?

25 "There was once a fisherman and his wife who drank themselves to death!"
Could you read it? And was it more difficult to read the 2nd one? Because we tend to read better when openings are revealed, rather than closings. Here goes, "Make hay while the sun shines."

"Books can be dangerous. The best ones should be labelled, 'This could change your life'."

– Helen Exley[26]

26 Helen Exley is a specialist gift book creator. She has curated over a thousand books of quotations since 1996.

CHAPTER 5

BOOKS, LIKE FRIENDS, MAKE OUR LIVES RICHER

As shared in my personal note, I wanted to be completely isolated in school and college to avoid the question "What does your father do?" However, ironically, the identity I crafted as 'the girl who reads' was in high demand.

Ever heard of group projects?

These are the norm, whether you're studying or working. Now whenever the teacher announced a group project, I would have at least five different groups fighting to have me in theirs. Whether the topic was the 10th planet or the extinction of dodos, everyone was sure I would know something about the subject and would offer to do the lion's share of work. High handed and officious for sure, but I would do it. Not only was this wonderful for my self-esteem, but it also egged me on further. Because only I knew how much I hustled beneath the surface, while appearing to be a calm 'all-knowing' creature outside.

This was the 1980s; so pre-Google times. I was armed with:

- Being a member at several lending libraries.

- *Raddiwalas*[27] along the path from home to school let me borrow old secondhand books if I gave them one in exchange.

---

27 Used paper and magazine vendors.

- The school library itself (that no one seemed to frequent enough)!

So, even if I was blind as a bat about a subject on Friday evening, by Monday morning I would see the subject clearly. The very act of reading had become a superpower and social lubricant for me!

Several years later, during one of the Reading Coach sessions, I stumbled upon another social benefit to reading. I was asked a very important question. Suresh Kumar, aged 27, an IT professional, asked, "I've always wanted to be popular. It's the one thing I've craved. Any way reading can help me? I've tried reading the classics before, but they seem like a drag!"

"You have a specific problem you want to solve. You should read up in a way that solves it," I said.

"How will reading change the fact that I am socially awkward?" he asked genuinely.

I answered his question with another question. "Why do you think you're not popular?"

"Because I can't seem to think of the right thing to say at the right time," he said. "I am tongue-tied. But very intelligent sentences come to my mind after the situation is over and everyone has gone home." Suresh was evidently frustrated.

"What you're going through is called the 'spirit of the stairs'. It's very common. People leave a meeting tongue-tied, only to go down to the end of the staircase and suddenly remember all the witty things they wish they had said. Such behavioural patterns are covered in several books," I responded.

Suresh seemed to warm up a little. I continued.

"In fact, there's a book titled *The Fine Art of Small Talk* by Debra Fine that you must read. In fact, Debra writes in the book that she chose to become an engineer, only so that she wouldn't have to talk to people! From that point to her eventual journey to become a communications coach, render her insights unique!"

"At least you've suggested a new book. I've been asked to read *How to Win Friends and Influence People* so many times that I hate it even without reading it!"

"That's a very important book too! But sometimes, you need a story similar to yours to relate to. I think we can safely say that Shakespeare is one of the world's most important writers; but not everyone reads his plays either. So you have to find a book that's right for you!"

Suresh's follow-up question was the real masterstroke! "So I read this book, and will it be enough?"

"No. I can offer no such guarantee. But it will get you started. You may like *How to Talk to Anyone* by Leil Lowndes. Maybe you will decide to take a new course, egged on by what you read. You can also try *The Charisma Myth: How Anyone Can Master the Art and Science of Personal Magnetism* by Olivia Cabane. Regardless, you will be on the path. Here's one thing I can guarantee; there's nothing that comes even close to reading, when it comes to conversation starters. Readers initiate more meaningful conversations than non-readers and are also able to hold the attention of people for longer!"

Is that a thing?

"Yes! Readers have more empathy and reference points that draw from that empathy. So they end up saying more 'connected' things that make conversations last longer!"

Suresh smiled. I was happy.

Picture courtesy: Jason Poland's popular webcomic 'My Dad is Dracula' explains 'the spirit of the stairs' well.

CHAPTER 6 NETWORKS, EXPERTISE, COMPETITION

There is a famous saying in Tamil, *'Ulakam oru pustakam, atai paṭikkātavarkal atai patri eduvum terintu koḷḷa muṭiyātu.'* It means that the world is a book, and those who do not read it cannot know anything about it.

Similarly, the Jain doctrine of 'Anekāntavāda' helps us understand the value of reading. It states that reality is many-sided and has multiple aspects. It's also known as the 'theory of manifoldness.'

Explaining Anekantavada, Manish Sabharwal, co-founder Ashoka University and chief honcho of TeamLease, says that there are many ways to learn.

In his words, *"Learning happens through:*

1. The relationships we form.
2. When we put ourselves in roles and experiences outside our comfort zone. (I have an MBA from Wharton but being on the RBI board was my best classroom.)
3. By reading a diverse set of books, even the authors that we disagree with.
4. Travel and other experiences that push our limits.

Of the above, books are the ones that are most easily available to all and perhaps the most sustainable habit to keep up. They are also the most pocket-friendly and easily implementable way to learn. What's more – you can get started straight away! How else can you travel across experiences and time zones while sitting in the comfort of your house? And there is no need to wait for someone to invite you anywhere or to mentor you. You want to spend four hours with Jiddu Krishnamurthy or Elon Musk, just pick up their books! And then the next one!"

Makes a lot of sense! As you will see, Sabharwal's 'Anekāntavāda' gets beautifully subsumed in the HELP MATRIX[28] that we have developed at The Reading Coach.

By and large, the consensus seems to be that a productive work life involves having some kind of expertise. No matter what the sphere of work, a deep commitment to self-improvement is necessary and this may be served by reading, among other things.

In the knowledge economy, as opposed to the farmer or the shop floor worker who measure their output in produce and units, workers in the knowledge economy have to demonstrate their value[29] in other ways. The biggest ability is to be able to **think critically**, solve problems, and communicate effectively at the end of which you may undergo some form of performance appraisal. But way before appraisal by others, one has to appraise oneself!

In the words of Peter Drucker[30], this involves:

Self-knowledge: This includes understanding one's strengths, weaknesses, values, and interests.

28 Chapter 11
29 Chapter 4 talks about this.
30 Extracted from Peter Drucker's book *Managing Oneself* - which is about the power of self-management.

Self-management: When you know yourself, you can manage yourself by setting goals, making plans, and taking action.

Self-renewal: In order to keep contributing, it is important to commit to continuous learning and development, challenge yourself and acquire new skills.

The list of books on self-knowledge, management and renewal are worth a lifetime in themselves. From *Autobiography of a Yogi* by Paramahansa Yogananda, to *Inner Engineering* by Sadhguru to *The Law of Attraction* by Esther and Jerry Hicks, this is the list you would do well to read, regardless of your other areas of interest.

Developing the gift of critical thinking is of great value…

Meaningful achievement requires the ability to put in 'deep work'. Now if you're someone who is happy with the mediocre status quo, then maybe deep work is not for you. But the fact that you've picked up this book means that you're keen to go the extra mile. Deep work is nothing but 'focus without distraction', a state that can lead to critical thinking.

This is a term popularised by Cal Newport[31] and involves deliberate action in a sense. It requires you to get into a state where you quieten everything else and focus on activating that part of your brain that will consume and process knowledge to the exclusion of all else.

One of the best ways to do this is reading. Now there are steps to this:

- absorbing what you read
- looking for connections and ideas that are not obvious
- slowing down and applying what you read to the situation at hand
- reaching out to a peer or mentor's inputs
- referring to other material
- going back to what you've read
- making notes, etc.

A nice analogue workout for the brain, non-tech, super effective!

I love this anecdote where Elon Musk, the creator of SpaceX, Tesla, and Starlink, claimed that in elementary school, he read for almost 10 hours every day. When asked where he got the ideas for building rockets and how he learnt to make them, Musk once famously said, "I read books."

So is success about diligent hard work or sheer talent?

There's an interesting book, *Developing Talent in Young People*[32], which examines the critical factors that contribute to talent.

31 Calvin C. Newport is an American non-fiction author and full-time professor of computer science at Georgetown University. He authored the book *Deep Work* in 2016.
32 Benjamin Bloom, at the University of Chicago, 1985.

Analysing 120 elite performers in fields ranging from music and the arts to mathematics and neurology, author Benjamin Bloom discovered that the only 'gifts at birth' that correlated with performance (in sports alone) were height and body size.

Otherwise, all elite performers had only this in common:

- they practised intensively
- studied with devoted teachers
- were supported enthusiastically by their families throughout their developing years.

The results were as expected.

"Experts are always made, not born!"

More than 100 leading scientists agreed![33]

Since all expertise involves strengthening the mind, I am emphasising that 'reading' is perhaps one of the most important tools to become an expert.

33 They studied expertise and top performance across domains: surgery, acting, chess, writing, computer programming, ballet, music, aviation, firefighting, and many others. Their conclusions are compiled in a 900-page-plus *The Cambridge Handbook of Expertise and Expert Performance*, Cambridge University Press, 2006 by K. Anders Ericsson

CHAPTER 7 YOU ARE THE COMPANY YOU KEEP!

Growth and progress, almost synonymous in the context we are using them here, are essential to life. And one of the most prolific writers about personal growth is Tony Robbins. Here's something he said about how our identity shapes our progress!

"The strongest force in the whole human personality is the need to stay consistent with how we define ourselves" – Tony Robbins

How do you define yourself? A go-getter? A progressive person? An agile learner who makes the most of the opportunities that are presented to them? Someone who proactively finds solutions to their problems instead of sitting around and moping about them?

No matter what the problem, the solution can potentially be found between the pages of a book. Whether it's through fictional characters or real-life experiences, books are the things to turn to whenever you need some wise advice that would change your life. Books make you aware of what the characters did in a similar situation and you emerge as a stronger person. Self-help books may also be strong

triggers to seed change.

Coming back to identity, and how we define ourselves, this has a deep impact on our friendships as well.

If you hang around five confident people, you will be the sixth.

If you hang around five intelligent people, you will be the sixth.

If you hang around five idiots, you will be the sixth.

Here's the catch. Reading more doesn't make us necessarily wiser! It is the quality of books that matters – reading better that makes us better.

Not all readers are equal.
I repeat, not all readers are equal!

An addictive reader of violent virulent pornography for example, can lead a couch life, eating deep fried pakodas[34], have no friends, no social connections, never do any physical activity or have any productive occupation. This is not what we are talking about here. In the same way, having more number of friends to count doesn't necessarily enrich our lives. The quality and authenticity of our friendships, and their routines and motivations, is the key.

At this point, we must define better books! I have come across people who classify books as 'fat' or 'thin', which frankly is extremely reductive. But there is such a thing as 'quality'; veteran journalist Purba Dutt explains how to determine this.

- Investigate the authenticity of the publisher-author combination.

34 Bengal gram fritters

- Investigate previous works by the author.
- Investigate the depth of research put into the book.
- Look for unpaid reviews.
- Give a first-time author the benefit of word of mouth.
- Check beyond books to study the author's blogs, TED talks, interviews, follower base, columns, etc
- Attend reading sessions by the author and find out your interest level.

A good book is a great friend. And therefore, you want to be sure you're making the right friend! Manish Sabharwal explains, *"Books are like your friends; you have a friend you work out with, a friend you gossip with and the friend you have dinner with."*

Variety in friendships is enriching. Similarly, variety in books:
- means a vast range of non-homogenous literature
- is essential to expand our minds. If you are reading about politics, you must read all sides to form a balanced view. Reading the same kind of books with the same opinions may end up reinforcing biases and prejudices.

Further, making reading a part of your routine is the key. The magic of routines is extolled by many authors; from Swami Vivekananda's many writings to Ryan Holiday's *Discipline is Destiny* to *The Greatness Mindset* by Lewis Howes, several authors talk about the value of habits and routines, so make sure you read those books.

Just as friendships build our emotional bank balance, 'reading good books' builds our intellectual as well as emotional bank balance. We can then apply this focus and emotional resilience in all other areas of life.

EXPERT READER ESSAY - 2

FIRST YOU LEARN TO READ, THEN YOU READ TO LEARN

I have read a book a week for 35 years. I have a two-storey library, flush with 12,000 books nesting at my home in Bengaluru. I built my house around the library, not the other way around.

At an early age, I was taught that reading is no different from learning. I was fortunate to have an opening balance in my 'reading' account – my parents read a lot. For any child, the presence of role models who are passionate about books is perhaps the best induction into the world of reading. Further, if these role models do not insist that you necessarily read the heavy stuff or the useful stuff and allow you to just read anything, you're all set!

As long as kids are reading, we have unlocked their curiosity. Books are most easily available to all and perhaps the most sustainable habit to keep up. Also the most pocket-friendly and easily implementable! What's more, you can get started straight away. How else can you travel across experiences and time zones while sitting in the comfort of your house? And there is no need to wait for someone to invite you to a challenging role or to mentor you. You want to spend four hours with Ratan Tata, just pick up his book! And then the next one!

Everyone is doing some kind of reading. Reading in the future will be even more important than literacy. Mostly because the latter is now more or less pervasive. **First you learn to read then you read to learn.** It's the responsibility of the educational institutions to inculcate the reading habit. Let's also zero in on what kind of reading we are talking about here. There is a lot of 'fast food' reading happening on our devices anyway. But the reflection that happens with old-school, long-form reading is safely absent from these modes of consumption. For sure, AI may be able to create the next franchise of a formula movie like *Fast and The Furious.* But can AI create something original and brilliant like *Shawshank Redemption?* I doubt.

On the flip side, if reading alone made us wise and well-rounded, academicians would be the wisest people in the world. But very often, academicians themselves are close-minded. In fact, anyone who choses homogeneous cognitive activities faces the burden of having a one-track mind. Because the most dangerous lies are the lies we tell ourselves. A lifelong devotion to just one kind of books can create that too!

For all my championing of reading, I know lots of wise people who are not readers. But as we discussed the doctrine of Anekāntavāda earlier, 'there are many ways to Rome!' Are educated people wiser than uneducated people? Not necessarily. Therefore, we may have to apply the 'doctrine of maybe' or 'Syādvāda', which is another Jain doctrine that all judgements are conditional, or only true in certain circumstances! There are a lot of intelligent people who don't read. They just choose one of the other cognitively diverse self-developmental experiences.

So, what is the challenge with reading? Why are people

weaning away from it, if such a thing were true.

Reading is a muscle. It's hard till it gets easy. It cuts through the rigidity of our own ideas lest they become our identity. Some read for breadth and others read for depth. Books are like friends; the friend I like to go out with to dinner is not the one I go out with for hiking. Also, people like to see themselves in what they read. In India, there isn't much literature that chronicles our history post-Independence. For all the beauty of William Wordsworth's 'Daffodils', my question is, 'where are the daffodils in India?'

Side note: As a reader, I find myself returning to *The History of Strategy* by Lawrence Friedman and *India after Gandhi* by Ramachandra Guha often. They question my thought process every time I read them.

Essay by Manish Sabharwal, *Vice Chairman at TeamLease Services Limited, co-founder Ashoka University.*

SECTION 3D
THE READING ADVANTAGE IN YOUR CAREER

Solution to mind puzzle 2[35]

MIND PUZZLE 3

Study the earlier sentence again

THE BINGULLY SHEP JUDED THE JINGULLY MEP

Draw a Bingully Shep and a Jingully Mep

35 THE BINGULLY SHEP JUDED THE JINGULLY MEP
And answer the questions
1. How was the shep? The shep was Bingully
2. Who juded the jingully mep? The Bingully Shep
3. How was the mep? The mep was Jingully
Note that even though you could not understand the sentence, you were able to answer the questions. Why is this?

Ajai Chowdhry[36], co-founder of HCL and the man who set up IIT Hyderabad, once told me that *he could identify a reader from a non-reader in a room full of employees, just by the way they spoke and the solutions they brought to the table. "The confidence is simply not there among non-readers!" he said.*

36 Essay by Ajai Chowdhry at the end of Section 3

CHAPTER 8 THE CONNECTION BETWEEN LASTING SUCCESS AND THE READING HABIT

Lasting success is the result of continuous self-education. Reading is one of the most proven ways to self-educate. Let's listen to those who attest to this.

"Successful men, in all callings, never stop acquiring specialised knowledge related to their major purpose, business, or profession," wrote Steve Siebold in his book *How Rich People Think.*

Modern women would ask, why is Steve Siebold only talking about successful 'men'? But the point he makes is moot. He goes on to write, *"Those who are not successful usually make the mistake of believing that the knowledge-acquiring period ends when one finishes school."* His observation is on the basis of several interviews with millionaires! Copy that!

Infosys honcho N.R. Narayana Murthy, has been an avid reader all his life. Interestingly, one of the books he recommends is *Winners Never Cheat Even in Difficult Times* by Jon Huntsman[37]. With vivid examples from the author's professional life, the book talks about how honesty and integrity are not only personal virtues, but can also be a good business strategy. Narayana Murthy is famously known to have augmented his wife and author Sudha Murthy's inclination

37 Hunstman was an American businessman and philanthropist. He was the founder and executive chairman of Huntsman Corporation, a global manufacturer and marketer of specialty chemicals.

towards reading as well, during their younger days. The couple is one of the shining examples of committed lifelong readers whose reputation and stature have only grown with time.

It should also come as no surprise that lifelong learner Steve Jobs stunned the world when he sold his book collection. Jobs privately professed an "inexhaustible interest" in William Blake – the 18th-century mystic poet and artist. How wonderful that one of the greatest, most visionary innovators of our time loved poetry!

In an article in Gulf News[38], Dr. Tommy Weir[39] writes about seeing Steve Jobs' book collection, *"I'll never forget being invited into one of those libraries; we spent an hour perusing through the CEO's 20,000 books. I was like a kid in a candy shop and mesmerised by what he read and how his growth was his private priority. As I think back on it, that hour with him and his books was a peek into his brain – what shaped him, what's important to him, how he thinks."*

What's more, reading is not just transformative for business owners alone!

Let's talk about one of the most decorated lawn tennis players of all time, Novak Djokovic. During the quarter final of the French Open in 2010, he lost to Austrian Jurgen Melzer after being two sets up. Post the match, Djokovic contemplated quitting tennis, *"I cried a lot after this defeat because I had a moment in my life, my career, when everything happened in a fusion in which I really did not see a reason to keep on playing, I wanted to quit tennis."*

38 Dr. Tommy Weir, Reading does make for an outstanding CEO, Gulf News, April 04, 2016
39 Dr. Tommy holds a doctorate in strategic leadership from Regent University, and is the founder of Emerging Markets Leadership Center (EMLC) where he is the region's leading CEO Coach.

Cut to 2011, Djokovic walked away with three out of the four Grand Slams in the calendar year. How did he transform himself into this emotionally resilient mental giant?

In a video released by the ATP[40] in 2009[41], Novak Djokovic revealed that his favourite book was *The Power of Now*, by German writer Eckhart Tolle. Later, while talking to American journalist Graham Bensinger on the latter's podcast in 2020, Djokovic spoke about what he learnt from the book. About how he had handled the difficult moments by practising mindfulness via meditation and journalling. He said that just being happy, joyful and present on the court, consciously focusing on his breathing and getting the best of the experience, helped him face break points and match points and execute them right. Wow! His great competitors Rafael Nadal and Roger Federer would have seen this in action.

In another universe, singer songwriter Taylor Swift has achieved unparalleled fandom. She has been vocal that the inspiration for her songs comes from literature. Pop music lovers credit Taylor Swift[42]'s success to being able to "relate to her meaningful lyrics" in a personal way. For example, her 2020 album 'Evermore' borrows inspiration from Daphne

40 The Association of Tennis Professionals, founded in 1990, is the apex body in the sport.
41 There is some anachronism in the example but one can safely surmise that he internalised the contents of the book over a couple of years.
42 Her favourite novels are *The Great Gatsby* by F. Scott Fitzgerald, John Green's *The Fault in Our Stars*, Harper Lee's *To Kill a Mockingbird* and *The Beautiful and Damned* by F. Scott Fitzgerald again! A good reading list there!

Du Maurier's classic *Rebecca.* Her 2014 breakup song "Wonderland" was inspired by Lewis Carroll's 1865 novel *Alice in Wonderland.* A young girl named Alice falls through a rabbit hole into a subterranean fantasy world populated by peculiar creatures. Swift uses "falling down the rabbit hole" as a metaphor for falling in love and losing your mind in the process. Deep!

Basketball great Lebron James, too, has openly spoken about his preference for reading. He has famously said in an interview[43], "I was reading to not only do something different, but to also take my mind off the game. Because during the post-season, everything is about the games. Everything is about the matchup and the team that you're playing and the city that you're in. I needed some moments where I could just get a different perspective – escape."

Readers seem to have an edge, no matter their vocation. Let's look at CEOs who read.

43 As told to Oprah Winfrey on an exclusive webisode: What's on LeBron James' Bookshelf? Season 1 Episode 135, Aired on 07/01/2012 | CC

CHAPTER 9 DO ALL CEOs READ?

Who is a CEO?

The person where the buck stops! The person who has to have a hundred eyes that see everything while **focusing their attention** on one goal at a time.

What is attention? William James, the father of psychology, defined **attention** as follows in the 19th century:

"Everyone knows what attention is. It's the taking possession by the mind in clear and vivid form of ONE out of what seems several simultaneously possible objects or trains of thought."

When explained like this, it makes sense. **What it implies is that attention is ALSO about "tuning out" information, sensations, and perceptions that are not relevant at the moment and focusing your energy on what is important. This is where it gets difficult.**

See, there is a competition between what you want to focus on and the distractions that prevent you from focusing on it.

Here's an example. During a targeted Reading Coach session, I had an exclusive audience of Executive Directors and above. Now they wanted to pose their questions one on one and not in a group. The CEO said to me, "On a typical day, I have five minutes to make an important decision in supply chain but tech-ops is already waiting to tell me about their problem. As the minutes tick, it seems almost certain that I'm going to miss my son's graduation. Just as I'm about to leave, the Industries Minister's Personal Assistant calls me over for a cup of tea! We had been working towards sharing our point of view with the Minister, about a legislation, for a long time. After 12-13 hours of crazy work, a lot of which is unplanned, where is the time to read?"

I asked, "Do you feel you're missing out on something by not reading?"

"Sometimes, yes! Somewhere in one corner of the world, some expert or professor writes a book or publishes research about our industry, some innovation that increases efficiency, which the shareholders bring up without notice in the middle of a meeting. I feel like an idiot, if I'm not aware!"

"They're just doing their job?"

"Yes, but I feel that my assistants should inform me about this before I go for the meeting! I should be the one talking about innovations that save cost or increase efficiency! But in the middle of one pressure situation after another, I can't even seem to remember[44] anything I've read either!"

"Good. You've explained your problem really well. It seems that you're expected to always be 100% informed; this is difficult and easier said than done. The other way is to react differently,

44 Many kindle users attest to the usefulness of the Readwise app to remedy this. Physical book readers benefit hugely from post-its that jut out of pages and contain pointers.

when a board member brings up a new book. Being 100% present, to appreciate the person while having the presence to 'recall' another similar book/publication, might be a better idea. And this emotional resilience is a gift that is given by the consistent practice of reading, among other things."

"You're back to reading!" He said exasperatedly. "I'm saying I don't have the time."

"I want to tell you what Mukesh Ambani famously said, 'I read a lot of technical stuff.... I read five or six things at the same time.' Ambani also routinely offers suggestions about the books he has read, such as *Big Little Breakthroughs* by Josh Linker, which focuses on the power of small innovations to create significant impact. Probably one of the busiest men in the world, Mukesh Ambani wouldn't possibly make time to read unless he saw value in it... and one can rest assured that he definitely knows how to extract the most from a book."

He laughed. "Why are you bringing Mukesh Ambani into the picture? I'm a small man!"

"The point I'm making is, you don't need to read a book end to end! Instead, read exactly to the extent that it helps you! Don't feel guilty about not completing the book and reading only the parts that help you! Can you start reading for six minutes a day? When you're answering nature's morning call?"

He turned pink but nodded.

"I guess I can find six minutes to read. But what's the logic?"

"There's research that suggests that reading for only six minutes reduces stress levels tremendously[45]! Let's begin there and see how it goes after a month!"

45 More details in chapter 26

CHAPTER 10 THE GUILT OF NOT FINISHING BOOKS YOU'VE BEGUN

It is not possible to form a lifelong relationship with everyone you meet! Apply the same logic to books.

"The number of books completed is a vanity metric. As you know more, you leave more books unfinished. Focus on new concepts with predictive power," says investor and thought leader Naval Ravikant.

What Naval is telling us is that putting in the time to get the knowledge advantage is an important function of reading. While I am not advocating 'book hopping', this is especially for those not starting to read out of the fear that a book once started should be read all the way through.

One of the best pieces of advice comes from the great Samuel Johnson himself.

"This is surely a strange advice; you may as well resolve that whatever men you happen to get acquainted with, you are to keep them for life. A book may be good for nothing; or there may be only one thing in it worth knowing; are we to read it all through?"

Pick the chapters you can benefit from and milk the most out of those.

Chances are that every author has something unique and important to share with you. Find that and revel in it. Because the more you benefit, the more you will stick to it. If you've crossed the threshold of what you can learn from the book, chances are that if compelled to finish it, you will drop off to a less cognitively rewarding activity.

I want to answer another question posed during one of my programmes. Similar to the CEO's question in the previous chapter, I was asked, "Seems like there's too much to do in a day. Exercise, eat healthy, spend time with 'real people', read. Isn't it too much to ask for?"

Here's the answer:

As part of a study on children, it was determined that reading **12 hours a week** is the optimal amount of reading, and can be linked to improved brain structure[46], according to researchers at the University of Cambridge[47] and their collaborators at Warwick and Fudan University in China.

Explaining this, Prof. Barbara Sahakian from the Department of Psychiatry at the University of Cambridge said, *"Reading isn't just a pleasurable experience – it's widely accepted that it inspires thinking and creativity, increases empathy and reduces stress. But on top of this, we found significant evidence that it's linked to important developmental factors in children, improving their cognition, mental health, and brain structure, which are cornerstones for future learning and well-being."*

However, beyond about 12 hours per week, there appeared to

46 Study Section 5
47 Sun Y-J, Sahakian BJ, Langley C, et al. Early-initiated childhood reading for pleasure: associations with better cognitive performance, mental well-being and brain structure in young adolescence. Psychological Medicine. 2024;54(2):359-373. doi:10.1017/S0033291723001381

be no additional benefits. In fact, there was a gradual decrease in cognition according to the study. This may suggest those children were more sedentary and spent less time at other activities that could be cognitively enriching, including sports and social activities.

High time we got introduced to the HELP matrix!

CHAPTER 11 ARE ALL READERS MORE INTELLIGENT THAN NON-READERS?

What do you think? Are educated people wiser than uneducated people?

My mother-in-law does not read. She has more patience, generosity and forbearance than anyone else I know and can solve more interpersonal problems than most. Hell, given a chance, she might've even changed Hitler's mind!

Like her, there are many intelligent people who don't read books.

I spoke to Alok Sama, author of *The Money Trap* and former President & CFO of SoftBank Group International. We had a little conversation that went as follows.

Me: Would you agree that non-readers lack the deep work skills of readers?

Sama: If by "deep work skills" you mean dedication, I disagree. My former boss Masayoshi Son is not a reader but is a visionary who works 24/7. I do believe reading, particularly literary fiction, enhances your understanding of the human condition which can be critical no matter what you do.

Me: Son-san might be an outlier. Because it's not just about dedication. The premise of "deep work" is the ability to focus for long periods of time, stay in ambiguity and solve a problem.

Sama: Son-san can certainly do that, and he is not a reader! Of course, he's an outlier. What about other entrepreneurs do "deep work" but may not be readers?

Me: Yes. Agree. They have other deeply immersive processes and some of the rustic ones never so much as open a book.

Sama: For me it's more about increasing your understanding of the world, of humanity. And of course being entertained!

Me: There will always be exceptions. However, for the vast majority of the masses, 'reading' is the cheapest, most accessible way to develop a vast range of skills, such as:

Inference

Deduction/Induction

Analogical Thinking

Imagery

Insight & Reflection

Background Knowledge

Perspective Taking/Empathy

Critical Analysis

Novel Thought

We are saying that when our young choose only scrolling over long-form reading, it may lead to shallow processing and convenient conclusions. They're not forming convictions of their own. This is a barrier to deep productive work that solves the problems of the world. Would you agree?

Sama: Yes all this makes sense!

So non-readers, take heart. Alok Sama, a man who knows Masayoshi Son really well, tells us that the latter is not a traditional reader. However, successful people invest in a combination of other modes of learning, within the hexagonal learning plan (we will call this the HELP matrix) below.

Picture 1 : HELP (HEXAGONAL LEARNING PLAN) Matrix

1. Practising empathy in the relationships we form.

2. Putting ourselves in roles and experiences outside our comfort zone.

3. Reading a diverse set of books, even the authors we disagree with.

4. Travel and other experiences that push our limits.

5. Committed pursuit of excellence in any realm: eg. personal fitness, a homemaker who unfailingly cooks nutritious meals for her family.
6. Any kind of spiritual immersion.

Let's face it, reading **'alone'** will not solve all our problems. It's not a magic pill but it's a great mode of learning that we MUST layer on other good habits.

Within the HELP matrix, our hypothesis is that people who follow any two of the modes of learning are on the path to self-improvement.

I know a top CEO, Aman (name changed) who is an Art of Living teacher (spiritual immersion as 1st mode of learning). He is thoroughly invested and empathetic (interpersonal relationships as 2nd mode of learning) and astoundingly insightful. And he's not afraid to rock the boat!

Rock the boat he did, by bringing his wife's mother to live with them. For the uninitiated, the joint family system in India dictates that the son's parents are taken care of by the son and the daughter-in-law. (The daughter's parents are expected to have their own son, who fulfil this function in turn.) Aman, however, insisted on taking care of his wife's mother when she contracted a terminal illness. He prioritised this over keeping his own healthy parents with him! His emotional anchor and his priorities were so strong that he cut through the clutter and did what was necessary.

I spoke to him about his decision and he asked me, "Reeta, have you read *The Death of Ivan Illych* by Leo Tolstoy?"

I had tears in my eyes when I heard Aman say this! In the book, Tolstoy writes about Ivan, who is terminally ill. During the long and painful process of dying, Ivan believes that he does not deserve suffering because he has lived rightly. So what was this senseless pain all about? He also begins to hate his family for avoiding the subject of his death and finds his only comfort in his peasant boy servant, Gerasim, the only person in Ivan's life who does not fear death. Ivan's own son and Gerasim are the only two who show compassion towards him; which makes him question whether he has, in fact, lived a good life! His sense of righteousness pales.

Eldercare seems thankless but is its own form of deep work and a great service. Aman received his mother-in-law's blessings amply.

Another very successful investment banker Sana learns music in her spare time. She has channelled her love for music into a purpose; her own band performs for charity. She does not shy away from all the reading that she has to do for work; but music has helped her overcome her own inhibitions; so much so, she loves putting herself in roles and experiences that challenge her constantly. She is in constant learning and feedback mode. She follows 'stepping outside her comfort zone' and 'pursuing excellence in music' as her two modes of learning.

Coming back to my mother-in-law, she is a classic example of a very fulfilled non-reader. She always puts herself last in all interpersonal relationships and I have not met anyone with more empathy. Her whole life has been about picking the freshest vegetables and fruits and making sure that everyone's breakfast, lunch and dinner is delicious. She has learnt everything from baking bread to baking casseroles to learning how to make the most exotic of pickles to keep her family happy. She is the most caring host when she throws a dinner party and will remember the smallest things that everyone likes. Her commitment to her family makes her a super achiever in my eyes! She's on two learning plans – interpersonal relationships and commitment to excellence in her kitchen.

However, there are days when everyone is at work and she feels lonely, when I can't help wondering whether reading could've kept her entertained. But more often than not, her emotional quotient overcomes her boredom and she finds something to do.

Dear reader, it's your turn to pick any two practices from the HELP matrix. I strongly suggest that you consider that no matter what you pick, make reading the 3rd mode of learning, if not the 1st and 2nd. It is a great habit that improves[48] our application of other habits.

48 Chapter 12 covers the decagonal benefits of reading

CHAPTER 12

THE DECAGONAL BENEFITS OF READING

The decagonal benefits of reading is one of the most important chapters in the book for obvious reasons. It applies not just to CEOs but anyone with a growth mindset.

Reading is an activity that promotes overall mental health. That's why the United Kingdom's National Health Service had begun 'Reading Well', a Books on Prescription programme[49], where medical experts prescribe self-help books, specifically for certain conditions.

We will also study in Section 5 how reading initiated a man-made evolution of the human brain.

But first, in this chapter, let us revel in its myriad benefits:

1. Constructing cognitive flexibility[50]: Research seems to suggest that cognitive flexibility – the ability of a person to shift a course of thought or action according to the changing demands of a situation – may be enhanced

---

49 Bibliotherapy is the use of books in the treatment of mental or psychological disorders. The Books on Prescription programme was developed with input from a range of partners including the Royal College of Psychiatrists, the Royal College of General Practitioners (RCGP) and the National Association of Primary Care (NAPC). From 2013 to 2015, Reading Well Books on Prescription reached 445,000 people with book-based help and support. After receiving a recommendation, the patient takes it to his or her local library where it can be exchanged for the book, although some people prefer to borrow the title without handing in the prescription. Books can be borrowed without a recommendation form. To access the list of books, visit reading-well.org.uk/books/books-on-prescription/commonmental-health-conditions reading-well.org.uk/books/book.

50 CRILS research team, Professor Philip Davis, Dr Josie Billington, Professor Rhiannon Corcoran and Dr Noreen O'Sullivan, conducted a series of experiments using functional magnetic resonance imaging (FMRI) to analyse the brain activity of 24 people reading poetry or literature with poetic effects. Since the sample size is small, further research has been recommended.

by reading. Reading allows an individual to abandon a previous 'set response' in order to generate an alternative response that is better suited to the situation at hand.

Napoleon Hill famously said, *"A closed mind stumbles over the blessings of life without recognising them."*

Experiments conducted by the University of Liverpool's Centre for Research into Reading, Literature and Society (CRILS) have found that literary reading could help increase cognitive flexibility. But only the right kind of reading.

Manish Sabharwal explains the dichotomy, *"If reading alone made us wise and well-rounded, then academicians would be the wisest people in the world. But very often, academicians themselves are close-minded. In fact, anyone who choses homogeneous cognitive activities faces the burden of having a one-track mind. Because the most dangerous lies are the lies we tell ourselves. A lifelong devotion to just one kind of books can create that too!"*

Which is why, from the get go, we have been advocating diversity of reading in this book – a mix of fiction, non-fiction, poetry and even picture books!

For instance, the CRILS researchers made their subjects read 'poetry' for the purpose of their experiment. One of the researchers, Professor Philip Davis explains, *"The research found that the sustained experience of reading poems might be expected to challenge rigid expectancies and fixed thoughts and to increase mental flexibility through the process of the reappraisal of meaning and the acceptance of fresh meanings, a process that was experienced as intrinsically rewarding."*

Now we know why Steve Jobs was fascinated by William Blake!

The openness to the idea that words have deeper meaning and being patient enough to discover multiple interpretations is the unique gift of reading poetry! Reading is known to improve neural function and mental flexibility.

2. Developing empathy: Reading is the original VR (Virtual Reality) experience for the brain.

Scientists have maintained that reading literary fiction can increase one's understanding of others and improve relationships. Fiction helps readers empathise with characters and learn their motivations and behaviour patterns. This is knowledge that carries over to life outside of a novel.

Reading about others' struggles with issues similar to ours, or otherwise, can be validating and help us feel less like a victim. The book *The Benefits of Being an Octopus* written by Ann Braden, tells the story of a young girl Zoey who has a lot of responsibilities. Not only does she take care of her younger siblings while her mom's at work, she also faces the additional horror of living with her mom's boyfriend. Zoey's goal in life is to be invisible, but such a stance is not sustainable. Eventually, Zoey cannot ignore things anymore and she has to speak up! In essence, Zoey strives to be like the 'octopus' in the title of the book – resilient and able to adapt to their environment.

Now when a young girl reads this book and sees how Zoey is managing her emotional upheavals, she finds the courage to do better and might find that her problems are infinitesimal as compared to Zoey. This can help her deal with her own trauma and adverse situations.

This can be understood better when we realise that, at a neuro-scientific level, when we read, the brain does not make a real distinction between 'reading about an experience' and 'actually living it'. The same neurological regions are stimulated, whether reading about a situation or experiencing it. That is why fictional stories can serve as a 'reality simulator'; they give us a chance to rehearse for interactions with others in the world, without doing any lasting damage to our experience of the present moment.

Furthermore, when readers select novels that are set in locations with cultures other than their own, they develop an awareness of diverse ways of life and perspectives. **Singapore-based Bhavani Krishnamurthy, founder of Kris Capital, explains this, *"Books have helped me hire better. I understand cultural contexts better and am able to pick up things like someone feeling bad about their origins or a potential trigger for difficult interpersonal relations at the workplace.***

I am also able to accommodate 'the unusual ones' better; for example, what is the life of a person in a trailer park in West Virginia? Is an IIT rank equivalent to one from the Royal Institute of Technology in Sweden? I also try to look beyond the obvious; how we judge people by the way they dress and the way they keep their houses. We readily slot someone in a socio-economic stratum without any nuanced thought. Reading has made me more sensitive for sure. When I meet someone new, I can navigate common interests better thanks to my reading and connect with people much faster."

3. Arresting cognitive decline with age: Regular, engaged leisure reading can strengthen memory skills in older adults, laying the groundwork for better practices in preserving our mental abilities as we age.

A team of researchers at the Beckman Institute for Advanced Science and Technology have discovered that reading may help preserve memory skills as people, and their brains, grow older. Their work is reported in **Frontiers in Psychology**[51].

The scientific explanation is this:

Reading builds episodic memory: This allows us to remember what happened in previous chapters of a book and to make sense of the ongoing story.

Reading builds working memory: This builds the capacity to hold things in our minds as we engage in other mental processes. Working memory helps us keep track of things that happened in recent paragraphs as we continue reading.

Both episodic memory and working memory tend to decline as we get older, but habitual readers routinely practise these skills in different contexts, thus keeping their brains sharper.

Singapore-based hypnotherapist and artist Nishtha Sipahimalani attests to the power of reading to arrest cognitive decline. *"My mum is a voracious reader! She is 90 years old and still reads late into the night. I can confidently say that a lifetime of reading has helped my mother bypass the cognitive decline."*

51 Elizabeth A. L. Stine-Morrow, Giavanna S. McCall, Ilber Manavbasi, Shukhan Ng, Daniel A. Llano, Aron K. Barbey, "The Effects of Sustained Literacy Engagement on Cognition and Sentence Processing Among Older Adults", Front. Psychol., 11 July 2022 Sec. Psychology of Aging, Volume 13 - 2022.

4. Committing to deep work: Reading is hard till it is easy!

The books you don't read cannot help you. That's why, if you choose reading as one of the habits to adopt from the **HELP Matrix,** you have to get to the point where you enjoy reading. Not everyone is a natural reader. Poor readers may not truly understand the joy of literature, but they can be trained to become better readers. And in this training, their brains actually change.

During a six-month daily reading programme from Carnegie Mellon, scientists reported that the volume of white matter[52] in the language area of the brain actually increased. White matter conducts, processes, and sends nerve signals up and down the spinal cord. It connects regions that send and receive signals, affecting our ability to focus and learn, solve problems, and stay balanced when walking.

When we stop identifying ourselves as non-readers, and switch to giving reading a chance; it can become a massively rewarding activity. And all we need to do is divert 30 minutes a day from OTT watching to a book on a topic we love!

With time and continuous practice, the benefits of reading start to consolidate, making it possible to stay in ambiguity longer and process complex information without anxiety.

Another aspect of this is the ability to build the 'focus' required for genuine, deep work. People interrupt themselves almost as much as they are interrupted by external sources. In her book *Attention Span,* Dr. Gloria Mark says that people interrupt

52 White matter is made up of nerve fibres (axons) that are covered in a fatty substance called myelin, which gives the tissue its white colour. Myelin also protects the nerve fibres from injury. White matter is located in the deeper tissues of the brain, while grey matter is found on the surface of the brain.

themselves about 44% of the time. Screens are not going away, and neither are other distractions. Distractions need to be understood, not simply avoided. We spend an average of just 47 seconds on any screen before shifting our attention. It takes 25 minutes to bring our attention back to a task after an interruption.

Reading steadies this crazy pattern of 'wavering attention' and allows you to put in the work that will actually elevate your contribution.

5. Developing emotional regulation: Reading is known to have proven benefits across interpersonal skills and pro-social behaviour. Reading can improve how we express ourselves, while we respond.

Think about this. If we were to see emotions and thoughts not as threatening, but rather as mental phenomena that are temporary, transient, interesting or at least neutral sources of information about our current mental state, we would not fear them, react to them or try and change them or expunge them immediately!

It is in this context that reading literally hits the ball out of the park!

What we know is that "reading comprehension is a constructive, active, situational, and strategic cognitive process, which is not only related to our language skills, but also closely linked to the development of emotional competence i.e. emotion recognition, expression, comprehension, regulation, and socialisation".[53]

53 Shiqing Wenren, Wan Ding, Zhenliang Wang, Yue Xia, Ruibo Xie, Weijian Li, Reciprocal effects between reading comprehension and emotional cognitive ability, Learning and Individual Differences, Volume 109, 2024, 102398, ISSN 1041-6080.

It is extremely beneficial to begin this process when young, because the neuro-plasticity[54] of the brain declines as adulthood progresses.

Reading helps us:

- Deal with ambiguity.
- While dealing with ambiguity, finding the words to rally people towards a common mission.
- Be able to listen to understand, rather than respond.
- Not be overly reactive. Reading nurtures the practice of reflection, making us consider possibilities rather than devolve to blame. Blaming others for our problems is the easiest thing to do.

This is an area where there will be much more research interest in the times to come.

6. Books are the greatest mentors: Reading non-fiction is arguably unparalleled in terms of cognitive development.

I can still have a few hours with Mahatma Gandhi, Sardar Patel and Rahul Bajaj if I read their respective biographies. And they are absolutely priceless. Broadly speaking, there are three ways to learn from other people.

a. To listen to audio books[55] or read books by and about people who've accomplished great things. (Audio books have

54 Neuroplasticity is the brain and nervous system's ability to change itself

55 David Daniel, a professor of psychology at James Madison University and a member of a National Academy of Sciences says, "If you're reading, it's pretty easy to go back and find the point at which you zoned out. It's not so easy if you're listening to a recording. Turning the page of a book also gives you a slight break." This brief pause may create space for your brain to store or savour the information you're absorbing. In Daniel's study, students who listened to a podcast lesson performed worse on a comprehension quiz than students who read the same lesson on paper. "And the podcast group did a lot worse, not a little worse," he says. Compared to the readers, the listeners scored an average of 28% lower on the quiz – about the difference between an A or a D grade, he says. Interestingly, at the start of the experiment, almost all the students wanted to be in the podcast group. "But then right before I gave them the quiz, I asked them again which group they would want to be in, and most of them had changed their minds – they wanted to be in the reading group," Daniel says. "They knew they hadn't learned as much."

28% less retention[56], says study.)

Thousands of successful people have written their stories in books. By reading their experiences, you can reduce your struggles by half AND learn from the mistakes of others. Imagine if I promised you three hours with Sam Walton or Akio Morita for INR 500/- or from your office library for free! What a steal!

No matter what the problem you're facing, the answer is out there in a book, only if you will look for it. There are books on every conceivable subject! From eating better to grooming better to finding a soul mate. Yet, people don't use them! How would you explain that? Baffles me!

b. Take someone you admire out for dinner and make them your mentor. Is this practical though?

Choose a really successful person and take him or her out to dinner, ask questions and listen. But can you take a rich person out to dinner? Do you have the money? Do they have the time? Can they be persuaded to come out to dinner with you? How will you contact this successful person? Besides, what are you expecting from this dinner? Is he or she going to drop ideas in your lap to change your life and multiply your income?

It may be true that poor people don't usually take very rich people out to dinner! This is an impractical idea!

c. Observe the routines of the person you admire

This is at least cheaper and more realistic than dinner. You can always watch what successful people do, because success leaves

56 Daniel, D. B., & Woody, W. D. (2010). They Hear, but Do Not Listen: Retention for Podcasted Material in a Classroom Context. Teaching of Psychology, 37(3), 199-203.

clues. Follow their interviews, what they publish and maybe even listen to their podcast or find another way to consume information they're putting out.

It may be a good idea to set up a HELP matrix fund for yourself; take a portion of your income each month and set it aside to invest in all the ways you can improve your knowledge. Remember the best money spent is the money spent to cultivate the genius of your own mind and spirit.

Make sure you don't spend more for accommodation than you do for education. The money may be small, but the promise of unlimited potential is real.

7. Stress reduction: In general, any meditative activity which compels you to focus on a single task can reduce stress.

A 2009 study at the University of Sussex[57] found that reading can reduce stress by up to 68%. It works better and faster than other relaxation methods such as listening[58] to music. **The caveat is that reading only helps reduce your stress if you pick something you enjoy that won't upset you. Reading the news may not be the best choice if it makes you feel angry or helpless.**

Researcher Dr. David Lewis, who conducted the 2009 study, explains, *"Reading is an active engaging of the imagination as the words on the printed page stimulate your creativity and cause you to enter what is essentially an altered state of consciousness."*

Pick a novel where you can escape into another world. Or

57 Lewis, D. (2009), Galaxy Stress Research. Mindlab International, Sussex University, UK.
58 Diagram on listening brain versus reading brain

read a non-fiction book about an activity that you enjoy – a hobby, travel, cooking.

Artist Nishtha Sipahimalani shares, "*I remember this incident vividly, from the time I was just a teenager. We were all at home. My mum and my older brother were reading and I was pestering my brother to play with me. He wanted to read, so my mum looked up from her book and suggesting that I shouldn't trouble my brother said,* ***'Read, because then you don't need entertainment'.***"

Scientists have suggested that 'giving your brain permission to disconnect from your real-life experiences' helps to ease muscle tension and causes your blood pressure and heart rate to decrease. This is also connected to 'better sleep' which is an extremely vital tool for stress reduction!

Imagine that it is bedtime and your mind is fixated on things that occurred throughout the day. Instead of watching television, reading before bed helps increase melatonin production by relaxing the body and dulling the pressure of the thoughts that keep you awake. Neurologically, reading is more rigorous for your brain than watching something or looking at an image. So you get tired faster and sleep well.

8. Reading and the 80:20 Rule: Would you rather spend all your time appreciating someone else's creativity or some time developing your own?

Reading books exposes readers to a diverse spectrum of concepts and viewpoints, which sparks original thinking and encourages creative problem-solving. As you read the words in a book, you create corresponding scenes in your mind.

You are free to convert the words into your own version of imagery. This develops your imagination.

But when you view visual content, you witness and appreciate someone else's imagination. There's nothing wrong with this and we must appreciate the art of others. But how would you rather spend all your time? **Spend your time developing your own imagination or work on appreciating someone else's?**

I suggest an 80:20 balance or at least a 60:40 balance, so that you spend a healthy amount of time working on your own personal development.

9. Encourages connecting the dots: Story structure encourages your brains to think in sequence, expanding your attention spans

Stories have a beginning, middle, and end, and that's a good thing for your brain, unlike the plain act of scrolling where you may land in an unstructured place without proper context. However, with structure, our brains are encouraged to think in sequence, linking cause and effect. Angus Fletcher, the professor who studies how literature can solve out problems, says, "The source of human intelligence is what we would call story or narrative, our ability to plan or plot, to come up with innovative answers to problems." The more you read, the more your brain is able to adapt to connected ways of thinking. And this is why the benefits of reading fiction are so underrated.

Neuroscientists encourage parents to take this knowledge and use it for children, by reading to them as much as possible. In doing so, you'll be instilling story structure in young minds while the brain has more plasticity, and the capacity to expand their attention span. Note that some of the most successful people around the world are good readers. They have an insatiable appetite for relevant knowledge; **they are driven to read because they just have to know!** Reading also naturally equips you with a better vocabulary and the confidence to hold your own in terms of content, within any discussion.

10. Reading perpetuates our evolutionary advantages.[59]

Summing up, personal development is the key to a good life. What you 'make of yourself,' the value you add to yourself, is the most important determinant of your fulfillment as a person.

Picture 2 : The Decagonal Benefits of Reading

59 More in Section 5

EXPERT READER ESSAY - 3

LINEAGE ALWAYS MATTERS WHEN IT COMES TO HABITS

I am a great believer in reading. Reading makes you think in new directions and this alone is invaluable! My preference remains physical books, even though I'm a techie at heart. I do use a Kindle in case of an emergency, if I have forgotten a book somewhere and I want to access it. Also, a Kindle can store a lot of books at one time which is a big plus!

My choice in reading has been mostly fiction. Days at work, building our business, have always been gruelling! Therefore, to read non-fiction at bedtime was too heavy! Nighttime reading for me has always been good fiction. I do prefer to catch up with non-fiction during my travels.

When I look back at my trigger for reading, I have to credit my brother! He is 10 years older to me and an avid reader of fiction; one of his favourites was Max Brand, who brought alive the popular fictional young medical intern, Dr. James Kildare, in his stories! He would come home during the holidays (college breaks) and sweep me into a whole new world of his thoughts and experiences. As I grew up, he also spoke to me about sales and marketing as a function and *Focus* by Al Ries and Jack Trout became one of my favourite books!

Here are five books that have had a deep influence on me and I think you should read them too!

1. I was deeply influenced by Vijay Mahajan's book *The 86 Percent Solution: How to Succeed in the Biggest Market Opportunity of the Next 50 Years.* It got me thinking, because the author said that *most global businesses focus nearly all their efforts on selling to the wealthiest 14% of the world's population. It's getting harder and harder to make a profit that way: these markets are oversaturated, over competitive, and declining.* I've gifted this book to so many people in the Government! The vision that global companies must come to India and make products for the world was a key idea shared in this book.

2. I also enjoyed reading *The Singularity Is Near: When Humans Transcend Biology* by futurist Ray Kurzweil. I met Ray at Bill Gates's house once and I was a complete fanboy! I went up to him, introduced myself and spoke about his book. I probably understood a lot more of his book than the lay reader because I was a techie! He was carrying 60 tablets in his pocket because he was doing work on 'how to live forever' which seems to be a favourite obsession of the rich! I also read his follow-up book *The Singularity Is Nearer: When We Merge with AI.* This fanboy moment made me realise that parents who hold authors in high esteem invariably impact their children to do so as well. We are a family of readers. In fact, I'm proud to say that my daughter-in-law has a 'reading class' with her children every day; where she and her kids just sit down together to read.

3. At one of the Nokia conferences, I encountered the Swedish author Jonas Riddlestrade who co-authored *Funky Business: Talent Makes Capital Dance,* along

with Kjell Nordstrom. The book talks about the idea of 'temporary monopolies' and explains that the way you succeed in business is not by having some kind of lifelong differentiator (because people will catch up!) but temporary monopolies. I have used this idea in my work many times without necessarily articulating it that way!

4. Another wonderful book I read is *The Two Second Advantage* by Vivek Ranadive and Kevin Maney. They talk about the ice-hockey legend Wayne Gretzky and how his brain made him exceptional. Over the past 15 years, scientists have found that what distinguishes the greatest musicians, athletes, and performers from the rest of us isn't just their motor skills or athletic abilities – it is the ability to anticipate events before they happen. This is what gives them the two-second advantage. I could immediately apply this to Sachin Tendulkar and see why he always had the two-second advantage too!

5. Once, I was travelling to Hyderabad to launch an IIT in the city as its Founder-Chairman. I met the great Dr. Ramesh Mashelkar on the flight! I told him candidly, "I don't know the first thing about how to start an educational institution." He was kind enough to advise me to read Clayton Christensen's *The Innovative University: Changing the DNA of Higher Education from the Inside Out.* In the book, Clayton Christensen and Henry Eyring decipher how universities can find innovative, less costly ways of performing their functions – another book that I read and applied to my work.

While on the subject of reading, I would like to mention the genius of Alan Turing during World War 2. There's a book *Alan Turing: The Enigma* by Andrew Hodges which is worth a read. He was a misunderstood genius whose contributions made the Allies win the war! Turing devoted himself to deep work. When he was 10 years old, he read Edwin Tenney Brewster's *Natural Wonders Every Child Should Know* and this made a big impression on him. Turing's is a classic story that trains us to look at success differently.

My input is that 'lineage always matters' when it comes to habits and I would like to encourage parents to show their children the path to reading books again!

Essay by Ajai Chowdhry, *co-founder HCL.*

SECTION 4

READING AND REAL LIFE

Solution to mind puzzle 3[60]

MIND PUZZLE 4

Decode this sentence

_ _ e_e _oe_ _ _ _ea_o_ _o_ _i_i_ _

60 MIND PUZZLE 3
Our ability to read and gather meaning draws from three elements: the visual, the syntax and the meaning. So the sentence, 'THE BINGULLY SHEP JUDED THE JINGULLY MEP', can be understood visually and syntactically but not by meaning. Therefore, you can answer basic questions like in mind puzzle 2 but not draw a bingully shep and a jingully mep.

"It is what you read when you don't have to that determines what you will be when you can't help it."
– Oscar Wilde

CHAPTER 13 READING AND RELATIONSHIPS

Reading is one of the greatest breakthroughs[61] known to man! Therefore, while picking your combination of two 'modes of learning' within the hexagonal learning plan (HELP matrix), make sure that you keep reading at least on the horizon as a third mode of learning.

Because readers might just save the world.

There! I said it. Let's understand this in the context of the wisdom in this wonderful book, *The Fourth Turning.* The authors[62] talk about how modern history moves in cycles, each one lasting about the length of a long human life, each composed of four eras that last about twenty years and that always arrive in the same order.

- Good times create weak people (who don't put in the effort)
- Weak people create bad times.
- Bad times create strong people (who put in the effort)
- Strong people create good times.

Every generation is convinced that they're living at a moment when the idea that "weak people create bad times" is on full display.

61 Chapter 17 covers the miracle of reading.
62 Based on Neil Howe and William Strauss' book by the same name.

Who are these weak people? And how do weak people create bad times? Perhaps a 'weak' person in this context may be defined as someone who is not committed to any learning modes within the HELP matrix. Who does not push himself or herself to be of value to society or even contribute to their own family. They are forever walking around with either a 'self-destruct' button or waiting to be offended. Know someone like this? Here's a story of how reading genuinely transformed a young man's life.

Rishi was a lovestruck Romeo I met a few years ago during one of my Reading Coach sessions. He had the eyes of a hurt puppy. He found a way to stay in touch on Instagram and in a very rare instance, sought a meeting in person.

Three things that defined his emotional state:

- Raha, the girl he couldn't marry *(they had been in love for more than a decade but their horoscopes didn't match),* was his identity. He was convinced that the whole world had conspired to separate them.

- He saw himself as a victim; someone who could not fulfill his love because of external factors. His parents were the villains.

- Despite his sharp mind, he would pay marginal attention to work. His dopamine system was about making Raha smile and he had not learnt the value of self-care in any manner that was separate from being of use to Raha.

Rishi would lash out at his own family, blaming them for separating him from Raha! I asked him, *"Weren't you and Raha both consenting adults above the legal marriageable age?*

You could've chosen to get married regardless the non-matching of your horoscopes?"

Rishi said, *"Raha didn't agree!"*

I asked, *"How are your parents to be blamed for that?"*

This stumped him!

Suddenly, he had no one to blame any more. I told him the story of Margaret Mitchell's *Gone With the Wind*. Raha, like Scarlett O Hara, was tough in parts but extremely fickle-minded and, possibly, very confused on her own.

Rishi was not a reader at all. He spent all his day moping about what could've been, projecting his sad state to anyone who would listen. A decade of love had left his cognitive powers woefully underdeveloped; thanks to the warped teenage notion that 'lovers complete each other.' Rishi lacked self-discipline, self-awareness, emotional regulation and perspective. In fact, we can explain most pitfalls of not being a reader through Rishi's behaviour.

1. They do not grasp fully the long term impact of their decisions.
2. They are adamant about their own world view. Any opposition to it is either quelled ferociously or disregarded entirely.
3. They don't have a solid grounding in any deep knowledge. They can be swayed easily by the lure of 'lower order[63] needs' over 'higher order purpose'.
4. They haven't developed their own north star in the direction of integrity. They may be willing to break rules at peril to

63 Maslow's hierarchy of needs

others, which makes them vulnerable to becoming smart crooks at best.

5. They are unable to overcome their cognitive biases to invest in a creative future.

Whenever we use the word creativity, we are talking about the application of time and energy to solving problems.

It was only when Rishi realised that he could look at his life in a whole new way, that he learned to take accountability. The book that made him see this was Dr. Wayne Dyer's book *Change Your Thoughts, Change Your Life.*

I explained to Rishi, **"The heart of reading is that moment when *'that which is the end of the author's wisdom appears to us as but the beginning of ours.'*** Marcel Proust said this. Let the wisdom flow unto you!"

Rishi is a successful entrepreneur today, complete by himself, living his life with a woman who is also complete by herself. They have a lot to offer each other!

CHAPTER 14 HOW DO I REMEMBER WHAT I READ?

During my sessions as the The Reading Coach, the idea of having people's attention is so precious to me that I muster all my energy to 'give back' a memorable session. Some sessions turn humorous thanks to the participation of my precious listeners. And so it was that in Bengaluru, an extremely well-groomed young man stood up to ask a question. The moment he stood up, there was a collective sigh from all the women in the audience.

"Is there a protocol to actually learn something from a book chapter? I used to highlight things, and I had a very elaborate system during my university days – it was a system of asterisks followed by explanations within pages. I would also insert papers with questions in the middle of pages. The question asked on the paper was answered in the page it was inserted."

"How sweet!" spoke a female voice who defied identification and the room broke into uncontrollable laughter.

Aryan Kohli blushed but he was quite comfortable with being eyed. So I asked, "Are you saying that your system is not working now?"

Aryan responded, *"For one, I'm not motivated to do it with the same rigour as before. For another, I didn't find the book very engaging. I would like to read a book about remembering what I read."*

"Our working memory[64] is very limited. Have you heard of the Ebbinghaus Forgetting Curve[65]? It shows just how quickly we forget information if we don't actively reinforce it!"

"Actively reinforce? How?"

"You do realise that technology has allowed us to outsource our memories. We don't have to remember anything. Many people add their friends' spouse's name, within the notes of a contact, to avoid remembering it. At the opportune moment, instead of asking, 'how's your wife', one can be more personal by enquiring with their name. We don't have to remember addresses, phone numbers, or any details searchable by Google. However, human memory is invaluable. *The Art of Memory* by Frances Yates could be a good starting point for you. For the benefit of everyone else, when you find something useful in a book, discuss it. Make notes and bookmark it. Re-read what you think may be useful."

"I could try that book," said Aryan. "But how do I go about reconnecting with my reading habit?"

"There are various ways to do this. Do you remember the book that made you fall in love with reading during your

64 Short-term memory is a component of memory that holds a small amount of information in an active, readily available state for a brief period, typically a few seconds to a minute. The duration of STM seems to be between 15 and 30 seconds, and STM's capacity is limited, often thought to be about 7±2 items. It's often likened to the brain's "working space," enabling tasks like reasoning and language comprehension. Information not rehearsed or processed can quickly be forgotten.

65 Hermann Ebbinghaus was a German psychologist who was one of the first to study memory and forgetting. In 1885, he conducted a series of experiments on himself to understand how memory worked. He would memorize a list of nonsense syllables (like 'ZOC' or'"KEF') and then test himself on how well he could recall them after certain time intervals. What he found was that he quickly forgot most of what he learned. In fact, after just 20 minutes, he had forgotten about 40% of the information. And after a day, he had forgotten about 70% of it.

childhood? Can you start there? The other thing is to use what you read and read what you use. The benefit of the outcome can motivate you." I asked, "What is it that you do?"

"Wealth management!" Came the answer. I asked him whether he had read Pulak Prasad's *What I Learnt About Investing From Darwin*.

"You see that's the thing. I don't want to read about work. Instead of reading another person's ideas about investing (even the great Pulak Prasad's) I'd rather read firsthand financial statements and form my own convictions!"

"Fair enough," I said.

"The other thing is, every time I search for a book online, I feel I am being marketed to. Authors are spending so much money online for self-promotion, that random names keep appearing out of nowhere. Everyone is a New York Times bestseller!"

The mood in the room was changing.

Another attendee stood up and said, "Hi ma'am, I'm Ruhi. Aryan is right. I wanted to read a book about negotiation skills and the suggestions that came up seemed quite basic to me! There was nothing about the author online, except for the one book!"

(This is exactly the reason why I enjoyed my sessions so much! People are so honest!)

A lot of the attendees echoed that 'good books were hiding behind bad, heavily marketed books!'

"I have a few suggestions! Yes, books are a business like any other, so they will be marketed! Let's not resent that. How will authors run their homes? That's their profession! Aryan, **many successful businessmen tend to read fiction at bedtime as a way to give their creative juices a boost. They say it helps them supercharge for the next day. Their daily workload is too heavy for non-fiction!** Good works of fiction are a great stress buster. You can choose good fiction set in the financial world perhaps? Ruhi, for negotiation, I suggest any book by William Ury. *Getting to Yes* is a fantastic book."

Ruhi made a note, even as Aryan said, "Fiction! What a waste of time!"

"Aryan, this is the most common misconception! Fiction has multiple benefits. Let's come back to your original question. Reading does not motivate you like before. Right?"

"Yes!" Aryan nodded.

"Treat your return to the reading habit as interval training. For the first week, read five days for 10 minutes each. In the second week, read five days for 15 minutes each. In the third week, read five days for 20 minutes each. Keep up the consistency and make it really bite-sized. Try Stephen Frey: he has written many books of fiction set in the financial world. Are you willing to try this?"

Aryan was happy to give it a shot and seemed to settle for the moment.

CHAPTER 15

RECIPE BOOKS, FLAT CAKES, AND YOUTUBE

Another day, another session.

The Reading Coach sessions are intimate and personal. **The idea of reading genuinely appeals to people and is on most of our to-do lists! We want to commit to reading immediately and almost feel guilty that we don't reach as much as we potentially can.**

During a session in Chennai, Shanthi Rajagopal, a marketing professional who was frustrated with her attempt to read a recipe book and bake a cake, decided to get up and tell me how useless cookbooks are!

"I made a list of my equipment and my ingredients. I followed the steps. And yet my cake was flat! Two hours down the drain and expenses to boot!" lamented Shanthi.

So I asked her three questions.

a. Did you follow each and every direction and not all of them in general? Often, baking a great fluffy cake is about the really small things.
b. Were you doing another activity at the time, while you were baking the cake?
c. Did you attempt any shortcuts?

Her face fell slightly but I admired her bravery. She answered,

"I was quite excited about the baking itself! So I was making calls to tell people that I was baking. I also shared pics of the steps I followed with a few people on WhatsApp. Somewhere in the middle, I also put clothes into the washing machine. So yeah, I might've missed one teeny weeny step!"

I was completely in awe of Shanti's honesty. So I said, "Please go on!"

"I guess, I felt so good about the open recipe book in front of me and the very idea of this wonderful cake, that I might've put the cart before the horse! There were times when I was glancing at the instructions from the corner of my eye, while also making sure that the minute *Bridgerton's* new season released at 3 pm, I would be the first to watch it! Another part of me was considering a future career as a baker. So I started scrolling the Instagram accounts of bakers randomly too!"

The entire crowd burst into laughter! And the best part was that Shanthi laughed too!

I asked the room, "Does everyone here remember an exercise called reading comprehension that we had school? We had to read a passage carefully and answer reasonably simple questions?"

The room nodded.

"But the questions are normally tricky. You have to read every word carefully, without being distracted, to get full marks in the comprehension!" chimed in one participant.

I told Shanthi, "I think your colleague has just answered why your cakes are flat!"

Shanthi understood!

I asked a follow-up question. "What is wrong with baking the cake by watching a YouTube recipe? Baking is a very functional, step-based activity and not so much a cognitively heavy pursuit. For example, if you want to work out, you may want to watch a video and follow the steps rather than read a book and work out."

This led to a very animated discussion on what should be learnt from YouTube and what should be learnt from books!

On the following weekend, Shanthi promised that she would give her 'focused' attention to the recipe.

I received a picture of a fluffy cake on Instagram a few days later. This time, it took Shanthi under one hour.

"Multi-tasking[66] is so overrated," Shanti texted me later!

66 Study Chapter 28.

CHAPTER 16 THE 60,000 THOUGHTS CROWDING YOUR BRAIN EVERY DAY

We experience around 60,000 thoughts per day! That's a lot. Our minds are constantly in motion, processing information, solving problems, and reacting to stimuli. Estimates suggest that a highly educated person in the 18th century would have consumed 74 gigabytes of information in their lifetime. The modern human being consumes this in a single day in 2024. Is our brain ready for this?

It's true that our brains are designed to handle vast amounts of information. To process this, the brain needs cognitive resources like:

Working memory: The ability to hold information in mind while performing other mental operations on the information.

Episodic memory: This is the ability to recall past events – read in previous chapters, other books or from our own life and relate them to the present moment.

Long-form reading of books is known to enhance both working memory and episodic memory. However, scrolling mindlessly and skimming digital environments for sensational news (given the information overload across devices) exceeds our cognitive capacity. Neither can our working memory hold it, nor can our episodic memory pause and relate to it.

Reading books is like a pause. It quietly injects fresh ideas into your mental stream. In a session I conducted for a group of HR professionals, I spoke about repetitive thoughts. "You will get the same 60,000 thoughts, day after day after day, if you don't inject fresh ones into your mental map by taking up deep practices like reading!"

A young girl Saba asked, "How do I know which book has life-changing ideas and which one doesn't?"

There are multiple ways to do this, I said. "Do you have a subscription to something called the 'Next Big Idea' club? It is actually a book club curated by authors Malcolm Gladwell, Adam Grant, Susan Cain, and Daniel Pink. It's a good starting point. Another could be to visit bookstores routinely and check out what is selling. A third could be to make it a habit to follow newspapers for the reviews of important books or a podcast like 'Overdue' that discusses books and authors."

Saba, "So this will help me transform my career?"

"Depends on the process you follow. We are continuously absorbing information and responding to it. While this flow of thoughts is necessary for processing our surroundings and staying adaptive, it also can become repetitive, locking us into fixed ways of thinking. Reading provides a unique opportunity to step outside the confines of our immediate environment and engage with ideas that may never have occurred to us otherwise."

"That's true. I can't get over this book I read called *Range* by David Epstein. In a world that celebrates specialists, he talks about generalists!"

"There you go! The stories we read, the characters we meet, and the concepts we explore allow us to stretch our mental boundaries and stimulate cognitive pathways that might otherwise remain dormant. This has the potential to influence our biology at a deeper level, including our genes," I said.

Saba looked at me as if I'd gone nuts! "Genes?"

"Yes. The impact of reading goes beyond its ability to generate ideas. In recent years, the field of epigenetics has shed light on how experiences, including intellectual stimulation, can physically alter our biology, even at the level of our genes. Genes don't do anything until they're expressed. The trigger that expresses them is our mind," I shared.

"Okay! What is epigenetics?" Saba was keen!

"Epigenetics studies how environmental factors can turn genes on or off. It explains why reading can help us reimagine our capabilities. When we read stories of individuals who have overcome adversity, achieved greatness, or defied the odds, we rethink what is possible in our own lives. This mindset shift has the potential to activate new neural pathways, fostering a belief in personal growth and achievement. Whether it's the idea of learning a new skill, changing careers, or pursuing a long-forgotten dream, reading helps us tap into a deeper sense of possibility!"

Saba smiled. I think the first book she is most likely to read is about epigenetics, not HR!

CHAPTER 17 APPLYING KNOWLEDGE

A 45-year-old CEO Ram told me once after a session that even though he was once an avid reader, he now prefers podcasts over books.

In his words, *"If I don't have a call scheduled while driving from point A to point B, I tune into a podcast. Of course, I realise that I may not give it 100% focus, and I may be answering WhatsApp or attending to emails, but it's a great use of my time."*

"Yes, podcasts are great. You're listening to something of immense value, when it's information that you don't have to 'apply end-to-end' yourself."

"What do you mean?" he asked.

"Imagine a medical student studying about how to operate on a patient! Would you rather they read it from a book and saw a senior doctor demonstrate it too and then performed it themselves, rather than just listen to it on a podcast?" I asked.

"I hadn't thought of it that way. Yes, your profession requires deeper study. But what about the time-saving aspect?"

"Not just medicine. You cannot become a lawyer by listening to podcasts either!" I said.

"But what if I just wanted to listen to an interview? Like

Dr. Ramakanta Panda on Shubhankar Mishra's podcast," Ram asked.

"Why not? Podcasts are a great trigger for further action. So if you're listening to an investor talking about looking for the next big investment opportunity, you may want to pitch to them yourself. But, you will have investigate/research their interest deeper before you actually reach out with an actual proposal."

"Yes. I remember listening to the benefits of eating raw food one day and then ended up reading a book on it to create my own 'raw food diet plan'!" Ram confessed.

"Podcasts are so much better than mindless browsing of reels! The other area where podcasts and audio books really work is that human beings have been sharing information orally for tens of thousands of years. Even before we started reading. Listeners can derive a lot of information from a speaker's inflections or intonations. For example, sarcasm, empathy etc. are much more easily communicated via audio than printed text. That's why we feel so connected to good podcasters! Besides, audio books are particularly advised for fiction in particular."

"But I'm not interested in listening to any fiction! I prefer business interviews and non-fiction only," Ram insisted.

"That's your choice. But audio books and podcasts ONLY exist because they add value. They are here to stay. There are all kinds of e-books and material that people are reading off their laptop. But here's what science is saying:

1. As audio books are a form of multitasking[67], we comprehend

67 Dr. Jennifer Davis, a clinical neuropsychologist and associate professor of psychiatry in The Warren Alpert Medical School of Brown University says, "Many people mistakenly believe that multitasking reflects a high level of cognitive ability and think that you should multitask to maintain your brain

and retain more when we read books rather than listen. If you're trying to learn while doing two things, you're not going to learn as well as you can when focused. Even the simplest of activities, like doing the dishes or the laundry, take up enough of your attention to create a barrier to learning.

2. David Daniel[68], a professor of psychology at James Madison University and a member of the National Academy of Sciences, co-authored a 2010 paper in which students who listened to a podcast lesson performed worse on a comprehension quiz than students who read the same lesson on paper. "And the podcast group did a lot worse, not a little worse," he says. Compared to the readers, the listeners scored an average of 28% lower on the quiz – about the difference between an A or a D grade, he says.

3. Paper reading is proven to be superior by several neuroscientists and theorists too. Carr[69] (2010) explored the effect of increased online reading on the human brain. He proposed that the ability to read deeply enables students to integrate memorised information into knowledge.

Carr identified the language and visual ability areas of the brain that were stimulated when reading print. **In addition to these, the decision-making and pattern analysis areas of the brain were also stimulated when reading online. This over stimulation may negatively affect readers' ability to reflect, absorb and recall information as effectively**

health (i.e., use it or lose it idea). In reality, our brains are not set up to multitask. We are designed to be "monotaskers," that is, to focus on and complete one task at a time."

68 Daniel, D. B., & Woody, W. D. (2010). They Hear, but Do Not Listen: Retention for Podcasted Material in a Classroom Context. Teaching of Psychology, 37(3), 199-203.

69 Nicholas G. Carr is an American journalist and writer who has published books and articles on technology, business, and culture. His book *The Shallows: What the Internet Is Doing to Our Brains* was a finalist for the 2011 Pulitzer Prize in General Nonfiction

as information in the paper form. As the brain becomes accustomed to reading less deeply from the screen, Durant and Horava (2015) question the negative effect on the development of deep reading skills and the richness of writing that may follow!

4. When similar research is conducted between ebooks and audiobooks, the difference is not so much. Beth Rogowsky, an associate professor of education at Bloomsburg University of Pennsylvania performed a study in 2016. One group in her study listened to sections of *Unbroken,* a non-fiction book about World War II by Laura Hillenbrand, while a second group read the same parts on an e-reader. She included a third group that both read and listened at the same time. Afterward, everyone took a quiz designed to measure how well they had absorbed the material. They found no significant differences in comprehension between reading, listening, or reading and listening simultaneously.

Ram nodded and asked, *"We cannot change the fact that more and more people are going to read online! Are we saying we could ask them to read books too?"*

"I agree! This concerns me immensely! Because when it comes to deep work, reading on print[70] trumps all else!" I responded.

"Modern researchers will find this unsustainable! My own daughter Ramya is a researcher. She cannot thank Google

70 For example, students scored lower in reading comprehension tests after reading a text presented on screen compared with paper (Mangen, Walgermo, & Brønnick, 2013). Liu (2005) found in a self-report study that when reading on screen, people tend to engage more in browsing and scanning, one-time reading, and non-linear reading, with less sustained attention and less time spent reading in depth. Such findings suggest that people perceive reading from a screen as appropriate for a superficial kind of reading. Indeed, Morineau, Blanche, Tobin, and Guéguen (2005) found that the mere presence of an e-book near a learner hindered recall of information, while the presence of the paper book facilitated it. They suggested that the medium on which a text is presented provides a contextual cue for the retrieval process. It is possible that because of this perception, fewer cognitive resources are mobilised for the comprehension and meta-comprehension processes when learning from a screen.

Books enough! It includes millions of books scanned from libraries and universities around the world – all accessible from her laptop!"

"Agree that Google Books is useful. But many of their books are available as 'snippet view' and you cannot quote them meaningfully till you've read the pages before and after. If Ramya's library is allowing full digital access of a book, it's extremely useful. It short shrifts the effort of finding physical books everytime. But, every once in a while, she has to sharpen the proverbial axe to cut the tree! One way to do this is to reboot her comprehension abilities by choosing to read a reference book offline."

"So, you're saying, do both?" Ram asked.

"Do we even have a choice anymore? Access to books provided by Kindle, Google Books etc., is phenomenal and it would be foolish to not make the most of them! But balancing it with non-screen reading gives the brain a much-needed break and boost both! Several researchers suggest that increasing exposure to technology – which is all about speed and multitasking – will end up making our processing shallower. This will compound into a larger issue of cognitive compromise[71] with time[72]. Similarly, podcasts too, might be a useful tool to supplement or enrich course-related material, but they are not as effective as text for delivering primary content."

Phew!

71 Duncan LG, McGeown SP, Griffiths YM, Stothard SE, Dobai A. Adolescent reading skill and engagement with digital and traditional literacies as predictors of reading comprehension. British Journal of Psychology, May 2016.
72 Pablo Delgado, Cristina Vargas, Rakefet Ackerman, Ladislao Salmerón. Don't throw away your printed books: A meta-analysis on the effects of reading media on reading comprehension, Educational Research Review, Volume 25, 2018, Pages 23-38, ISSN 1747-938X.

EXPERT READER ESSAY - 4

WHERE ARE THE PEOPLE WITH DEEP EXPERTISE?

My trigger for reading was my sister! Even though I was Harry Potter's age when the book first came out in the 90s, I somehow resisted J.K. Rowling for a long time, because I thought it was some kind of a fad. It was only when my sister picked up the book that I gave in. And while I was not prepared to become a fan, I was unwittingly hooked after Chapter 3! Thanks to our matching ages back then, I thought 'I was like Harry Potter,' and was mighty pleased about it!

Let us take a moment to celebrate J.K. Rowling's magical work; she made a whole generation 'hooked' to reading. I remember standing in line at 7 am in the morning to get one of the Harry Potter books! On another occasion, one night, my dad wanted us to do the dishes. He kept the Harry Potter book on top of the kitchen shelf as an incentive, "finish the dishes and then you get to read the book!"

My early inclination when it came to reading was towards fantasy; I enjoyed C.S. Lewis's *Chronicles of Narnia.* Then there was *Tales of Redwall* by Brian Jacques. I pursued my exploration of fantasy books to the deep end; so much so, that when *Lord of The Rings* came out as a movie in 2001, I wanted to read the book before I watched the movie.

Fiction gave me licence to live in a world where everything was possible and my appetite was insatiable. I loved the *Heir to the Empire trilogy* by Timothy Zahn, *Goosebumps* by R.L. Stine, and choose your own adventure books. Then there was *Unfinished Tales of Númenor and Middle-earth* by J.R.R. Tolkien, *The Delta Quest*, a set of eight books by Emily Rhonda. Ahead of my 15th birthday, my mom went to the bookstore and asked the sales representative to recommend a new fantasy series. That was the day I was introduced to George Martin's *A Game of Thrones,* eight years before the TV show hit the OTT circuit. I am proud to say that I was *A Game of Thrones* veteran by the time the HBO series came out!

This might be a good time to bring in that my mom's British; at one point, she started getting history books of the history of Britain home and nudged me in another direction when I showed interest in history in primary school learning about the Romans and King Henry VIII and his six wives. I became interested in Tudor history, ancient Greek and Roman history more. As high school ended, I was reading more of hardcore literature; such as the poetry of Seamus Heaney and Robert Frost. In the last year of high school, history and fiction – my two loves – seemed to merge together in the Dan Brown novels.

I'd never left Australia during my years of high school. Then my sister and I travelled around the world during my first year of university. Funnily enough, I thought to myself, *"It's a dangerous business, Frodo, going out your door. You step onto the road, and if you don't keep your feet, there's no knowing where you might be swept off to,"* which is what J.R.R. Tolkien had said in *Lord of The Rings.* I knew that this was a sign that I needed to keep my wits about myself, and this quote is literally on the first page of my own book!

Later, as I began to study law, I never imagined that the study of law would compel me in any way to actually practise law. M. Scott Peck's book *The Road Less Travelled* had a very deep impact on me around this time; the book talks about how honesty and the willingness to confront uncomfortable truths about oneself are the key. So I was prepared to not follow everyone else's path.

As I was figuring out what I wanted to do with my life, Paulo Coelho's *Alchemist,* in which he encourages us to 'follow our personal legend', was a gamechanger. My readings in science fiction helped me broaden my perspective as I progressed through university; I remember it was Isaac Asimov who said, *'Never let your sense of morals get in the way of doing what's right'.* Science fiction was really about the history of the future, and it's a genre I return to again and again when I want to be inspired – from Neal Stephensen's epic *Seveneves* to Kim Stanley Robinson's *Ministry of the Future.* It prefigures in many cases where we are heading and what threats and opportunities lie before humanity. I still return to fantasy every now again, however, including the classics of C.S. Lewis who wrote in *The Voyage of the Dawn Treader;*

"In our world," said Eustace, *"a star is a huge ball of flaming gas."*

"Even in your world, my son, that is not what a star is, but only what it is made of." This made me think deeply about who I was. Much later, as I started working in advocacy, political memoirs entered my world with *Tony Blair - A Journey* and Walter Isaacson's *Benjamin Franklin.*

I believe strongly in the power of reading. In fact, when the last Harry Potter books were out in 2007 I was much older and a friend said they read the summary off Wikipedia! I was genuinely saddened because they were missing out on a very well-crafted, immersive experience. That is what reading is all about.

I believe that 'lack of immersion' is part of the problem today; where are the innovators and where are the people with deep expertise?

We miss out on so many nuances when we don't commit to deep study. Yes, the benefits of a digital world are many, but we cannot overlook the fact that we must grapple with complex layers of information if we have to find solutions to the problems of the world. And books are a wonderful way to do that.

Essay by Michael Sheldrick, *founder Global Citizen.*

SECTION 5

UNLIKE THE TUMMY, THE BRAIN DOESN'T SIGNAL WHEN EMPTY

Solution to mind puzzle 4[73]

MIND PUZZLE 5

Complete the sentence.

"Though repulsive and stinking, the sewer......

73 Decoding the sentence where only vowels are given is exceedingly difficult. Because vowels are so unpredictable with the 'sounds' they make. Consonants are more consistent. Hence, one answer to '_ _e_e _oe_ _ _ _ea_o_ _o_ _i_i_ _' could be 'there goes my reason for living' a very famous song. There could be multiple interpretations.

"A book is made from a tree. It is an assemblage of flat, flexible parts (still called "leaves") imprinted with dark pigmented squiggles. One glance at it and you hear the voice of another person, perhaps someone dead for thousands of years. Across the millennia, the author is speaking, clearly and silently, inside your head, directly to you. Writing is perhaps the greatest of human inventions, binding together people, citizens of distant epochs, who never knew one another. Books break the shackles of time – proof that humans can work magic."

– Carl Sagan[74]

74 Carl Edward Sagan was an American astronomer, planetary scientist and science communicator.

CHAPTER 18 SOME BREEZY SCIENTIFIC TRUTHS WE CANNOT IGNORE

Why does reading have such far-reaching consequences in our lives? The science behind it is compelling.

We were never born to read. The first neurons appeared 600 million years ago. But reading began only about 6000 years ago because we taught ourselves. This triggered a reading helped homo sapiens rise above all other species. Reading, as an activity, is a neurologically and intellectually rigorous act. Once acquired and practiced, it brought along changes that were hugely constructive to the preservation of human civilization.

Hence, despite the rigour, we went ahead and learned how to read!

Neuroscientist Catherine Stoodley[75] at Oxford explains this and I've organised her observations in a diagram on page 112.

The very act of reading requires all sorts of new connections to be created in the human brain. Without being consciously aware, highly automatic rules take over the brain during the reading process. This means that **our brain has some kind of 'open architecture' within which it is able to rearrange itself to perform a new function!** Let's call this the brain's 'plastic design', which changes forever when reading takes

75 Catherine Stoodley is interested in the neuroscience of cognitive development, particularly the role of the human cerebellum in cognition, cognitive development and in neuro-developmental disorders.

place both at both the physiological and intellectual level. Refer to the brain diagram on page 109.

What is even more uncanny is the fact that this ability is very finely developed. For example, except for the few with specific neurological ailments, there is no confusion about which letter is captured here, despite all the different shapes!

No matter the shape and form, we are able to read the alphabet quite precisely. Similarly, except for those with specific neurological ailments, there is no confusion about what the following sentence represents!

EArLy HuMaNs coMMunIcAtEd tHrOuGh sYmBoLs[76] aNd GeStUrEs, BeFoRe wRiTiNg cAmE aLoNg.

And while this by itself is miraculous enough, it's just the beginning! Our mind puzzles explain the miracle of reading the best.

76 Archaeological evidence suggests that symbolic behaviour dates back at least 100,000 years, with examples such as cave paintings, engravings, and ritualistic artefacts found across various ancient sites. These early symbols likely served as a means of communication, conveying basic ideas, concepts, and narratives within ancient communities.

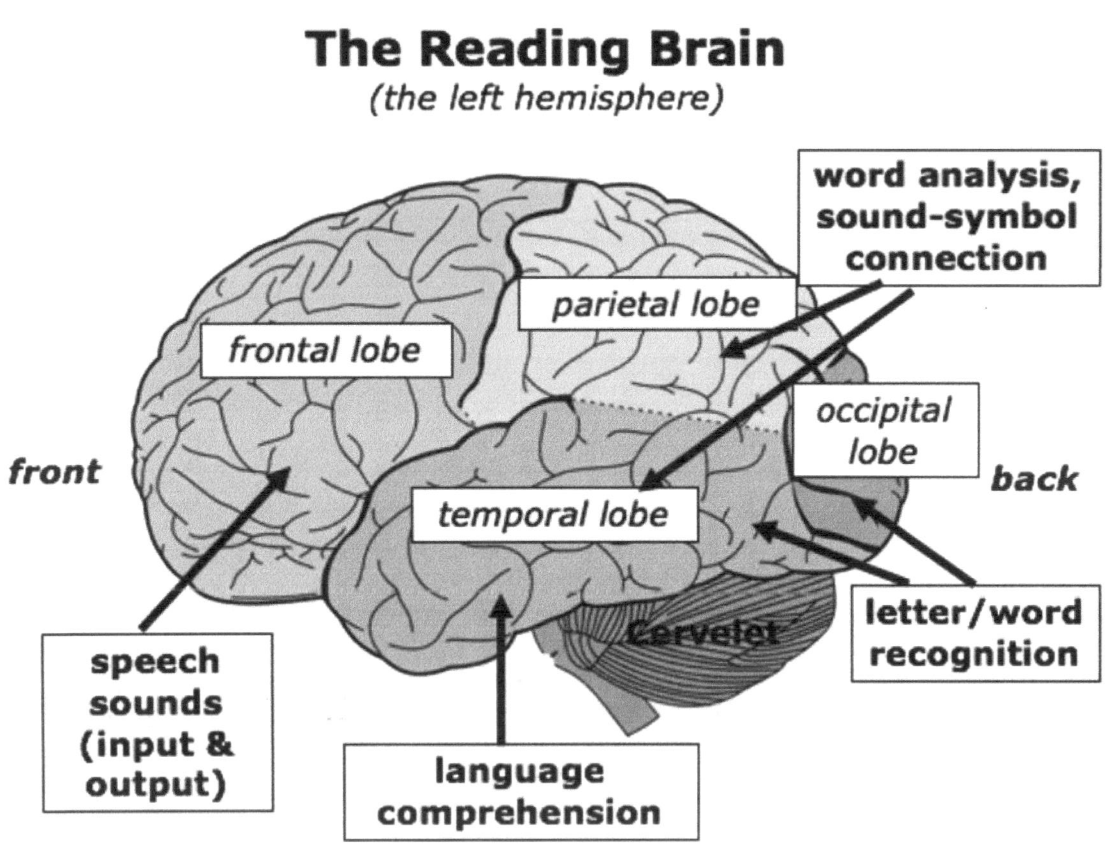

Picture 3 : The Reading Brain

Indeed, the human brain is complicated, and our understanding of it is constantly evolving – as are our theories of how the brain "works" during reading. But neuroimaging research indicates that the brains of typically developing readers undergo changes as they learn to read. As students receive reading instruction and then practise and apply these newly taught skills, they are able to "train" key areas of their brain to make it reading ready.

We connect what we read, to what we already know, and figure out new inferences. For instance, while reading a book, we make the 'leap' from our own 'life setting' to the author's 'life setting' – including their time, place, beliefs, prejudices, limitations and challenges! All of these could be potential 'triggers' that make a new 'connection' in our minds.

This then shapes what we think about and how we think about it. Which is why Joseph Epstein[77] said, "we are what we read!" And we have gained plenty of skills from the act of reading.

Reading results in a transformed mind and changed brain. It is *'generative.'* Simply put, it means that 'reading generates action'.

Reading leads to thinking.
Thinking eventually will answer a few questions for you and also pose newer ones.
This should be able to spark your curiosity towards further exploration.
During this journey, you will figure out what things mean to you and what bothers you.
Armed with clarity, you may be inspired towards a course

77 Distinguished American essayist, columnist

Picture 4 : Reading is Generative

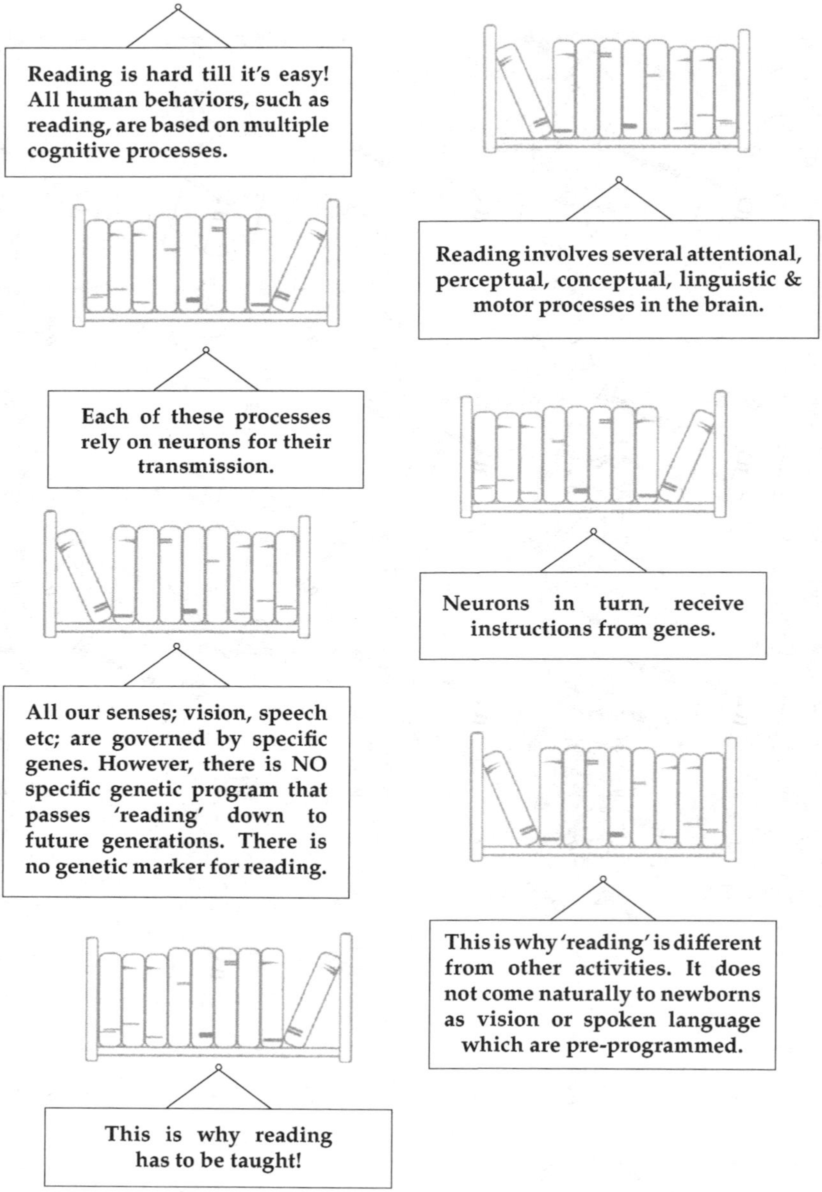

Picture 5 : Genes and Reading

of action.

And when you act in an informed way, you may creatively solve problems you were facing in the first place.

Now 'action' is extremely important.

Whatever you choose to act on is determined by your own environment and belief systems. A lot of basic assumptions and understandings are based on the environment in which you are raised. Let's call this the base of knowledge that every individual already has. Reading builds a layer of awareness on this base and activates creativity. Creativity, by its very nature, creates momentum for people to act in different, unpredictable directions.

For example, freedom movements around the world owe a lot to the rousing literature that was printed and circulated by revolutionaries, which generated massive protests and movements.

Let us therefore accept that reading is a key stage of evolution of human intelligence! And also, that we are in the middle of another evolution; the transition from a physical reading brain to an increasingly digital one. This will also have its own consequences.

The question remains – what new demands[78], if any, are being made on our brain, by the digital culture? But first – let's appreciate the miracle of reading fully!

78 Section 6

CHAPTER 19 NEWBORNS CANNOT READ WHEN THEY OPEN THEIR EYES

Let us delve into the order in which our five[79] senses developed, on the evolutionary scale.

Life itself probably first appeared ~3.7 billion years ago as a simple cell with the ability to replicate. In a manner of speaking, the very first organisms evolved in a chemical soup. They were free floating with no senses as we have come to know them, except perhaps chemical reactivity and sensitivity. And from this soup-like existence to multicellular organisms, the question of which sense came first has puzzled scientists. Touch is thought to be one of the first[80] senses to develop, using a variety of receptors in the skin.

There is another theory that taste is the most ancient of our senses, almost two billion[81] years old! It may also fit in with the free floating chemical soup understanding, given that taste is really just the ability to detect particular chemicals in your immediate environment! Ocean-dwelling bacteria were able to sense nearby nutrients and swim towards them at least two billion years ago! But sensing nearby nutrients while swimming in them also points to 'touch' again!

79 The nine-sense theory also has supporters. Generally agreed senses for neuroscientists currently include the following to the five senses.
a. Thermoception - the sense of heat (there is some debate that the sense of cold may be a separate sense)
b. Nociception - the perception of pain
c. Equilibrioception - the perception of balance
d. Proprioception - the perception of body awareness (close your eyes and touch your nose. Got it first time? That's proprioception in action)
80 Stanford Encyclopedia of Philosophy
81 https://www.sciencefocus.com/the-human-body/which-of-our-senses-evolved-first

Now, whether touch is the oldest sense may be under debate; but on an evolutionary scale, that 'touch' is much primitive/ older than sight is well-established. Neurobiologist Dr Liam Drew says, "Touch is our most intimate sense. Sight, smell and hearing evolved to understand the world at a distance, but touch, like taste, analyses objects in direct contact with our body."

What you touch is directly related to survival or reproduction. We place a huge premium on what we touch, be it a lover or an item of food. It defines what is most precious to us, like embracing family. It is also the first sense to develop during the gestation period, with some fetuses responding to touch after approximately eight weeks.

Babies are born with all five senses – sight, hearing, smell, taste, and touch. Out of these, except for sight which forms fully over time, all other senses are fully developed in newborns.

Regions of our brain and spinal cord are dedicated to processing the information gathered by touch. Given how powerful the sense of touch is, it is understandable that its impact is huge. This is one of the greatest arguments in favour of picking up a physical book, flipping the pages, making notes, feeling intimate with and connected to the reading process itself. Information is processed more effectively when multiple senses are used. Touching, seeing, feeling, even smelling the book, leads to more senses being used when reading a book. The text itself provides a 'landscape' as we read. This in turn helps the memory centre[82] become more active.

While we are on touch, we cannot leave the important question

82 Benefits of reading in section 3

of e-book readers unattended. Those who love e-books, please read them. It's better than not reading at all and provides several advantages, such as,

- Many books at a time
- Easy to carry

Which a physical book doesn't!

But, and there is a big but…

The 'spatial navigability' in a physical book cannot be equalled by Kindle. This is wholly tactile – a sense of the number of pages done and what's left to be done!

When holding a book, we have a tactile sense of the progress of our reading. And for those who love bookmarks, writing post-its, making annotations on the pages and all such things quaint, reading a book with a cup of coffee is almost like meditation. Further, the fact that printed text is anchored to a specific location on a page also seems to help people remember it better than screen-based text[83], thanks to the spatial attributes of traditional printed media. All this may be relevant to the audiobook versus book debate as well because, like digital screens, audiobooks also deny users the spatial cues they would use while reading from printed text.

One cannot therefore deny that the tactile component of reading has its own merits. Further, given that the ability to read is one of humanity's most significant achievements, enabling the transmission of knowledge, culture, and ideas across generations, touch only enhances this!

Daniel Willingham, a professor of psychology at the

83 Gemma Walsh (2016) Screen and Paper Reading Research – A Literature Review, Australian Academic & Research Libraries, 47:3, 160-173, DOI: 10.1080/00048623.2016.1227661

University of Virginia and author of *Raising Kids Who Read*, says, ***"As you're reading a narrative, the sequence of events is important, and knowing where you are in a book helps you build that arc of narrative. While e-readers try to replicate this by telling you how much of a book you have left, in a percentage or length of time to the end, this doesn't seem to have the same narrative-orienting[84] effect as reading from a traditional book."***

We have to accept, that with time, more and more people will be carrying e-readers along. We must first of all accept this as an inevitable sign of changing times. Many people read e-books; first up, it's better than not reading at all. In certain professions like research, there's the added advantage of access to a vast digital library of research papers, books, and articles from anywhere with an internet connection, eliminating the need to visit physical libraries

However, those who are raising their children to be deep readers must know why e-books are not 'almost' the same as physical books from a neuroscience point of view. Here are strong reasons to choose physical books while doing the customary digital reading.

a. E-reading reduces REM sleep

If you are introducing your child to read before bedtime, you should avoid using an electronic device. This is way more distracting than having a paper book because it reduces REM sleep! Rapid eye movement sleep plays a big role in memory, brain development, dreaming, processing emotions, and more. Electronic devices extend the amount of time that is

84 Another reason for this is that touch is a very powerful and primitive sense for us.

required for you to fall asleep. Sometimes, these devices can disrupt brain waves so much that you cannot stay asleep. People receiving less sleep do not receive enough REM sleep throughout the night.

b. Print reading is advised when reading for pleasure or deeper investigation

Most people today jump back and forth between physical and e-books. The convenience of the latter is undeniable. However, print is visually less demanding and tiring than digital text. It provides spatial and tactile cues to help readers process words on a page. Mindset may also be a factor. If people associate screen time with casual web-surfing they may rush through without fully absorbing the text – in psychology, this is called 'priming.' Studies[85] have found that digital reading breeds overconfidence. We read digital [text] more quickly, [so] we think we must understand it better. Scientist Lauren Singer Trakhman, who studies reading comprehension at the University of Maryland, College Park says, "It's one of the best parts of our digital world – everything is at our fingertips and we can get the headlines in a second – but it may also be one of the pitfalls. Everything's so quick and accessible that we may not be truly digesting [what we read] anymore."

By and large, digital is good to scan news headings for main ideas, but longer, complicated texts are best read in print, especially to retain the details.

c. E-reading slows down melatonin production

Electronics emit blue light when they are used. While some

85 Tirza Lauterman, Rakefet Ackerman, Overcoming screen inferiority in learning and calibration, Computers in Human Behavior, Volume 35, 2014, Pages 455-463.

of these devices have gone through many iterations of improvement, none yet have a 0% emission rate of blue light and this disrupts the body's ability to produce melatonin. Any level of blue light can disrupt your sleep, slow down melatonin production and should be avoided before bed.

Instead of an e-reader, if you're reading on your iPad, then the freedom to wander can destroy the whole sanctity and focus of reading!

The gatekeepers who are witnessing the transition from physical books to e-books are the readers who still love physical books. They must take a more active role as parents and as the community to save the reading habit. Of course, educational institutions, media outlets and influencers, all have to come together to make this happen! We sign off this chapter with a poem that celebrates the importance of parents to developing the reading habit in their children.

When Mother Reads Aloud[86]

— *Anonymous*

When Mother reads aloud, far lands
Seem very near and true;
I cross the desert's gleaming sands,
Or hunt the jungle's prowling bands,
Or sail the ocean blue.
Far heights, whose peaks the cold mists shroud,
I scale, when Mother reads aloud.

86 Severally attributed, the provenance of this poem is uncertain.

CHAPTER 20 32 MILLION WORDS SMARTER BY AGE FOUR

Learning to read begins the first time a child is read to! Here's a beautiful poem by Julia Donaldson to illustrate this point.

I opened a book and in I strode,

Now nobody can find me.
I've left my chair, my house, my road,
My town and my world behind me.

I'm wearing the cloak, I've slipped on the ring,
I've swallowed the magic potion.
I've fought with a dragon, dined with a king
And dived in a bottomless ocean.

I opened a book and made some friends.
I shared their tears and laughter
And followed their road with its bumps and bends
To the happily ever after.

I finished my book and out I came.
The cloak can no longer hide me.
My chair and my house are just the same,
But I have a book inside me.

No matter what the content that is read; be it a story, a nursery rhyme or even a prayer. Look around you. Clearly, there is much variation in the kind of experience that each family provides their child. Studies have shown that the very act of 'reading for pleasure' in childhood is surprisingly correlated to better cognition in adulthood!

Inventor Thomas Edison developed an early love of reading because his mother encouraged him to read anything that caught his attention. He loved reading books by his technological idol, Michael Faraday, and Thomas Paine, the literary patriot of the American Revolution. Edison also understood the importance of libraries and gave his staff members access to the most recent knowledge. He started this practice at his lab in Menlo Park and then moved it to the labs in West Orange, which are now part of the Thomas Edison National Historical Park.

Let's take a look at two important studies here!

1. What happens when the child is read or spoken to[87]

During a story-listening fMRI[88] task, children who had experienced more conversational turns with adults[89] exhibited greater Broca's area[90] activation, which explains the relation between children's language exposure and verbal skill.

This is the first evidence directly relating children's language environments with neural language processing. The study also found that conversational experience impacts neural language

87 Rachel R. Romeo, Julia A. Leonard, Sydney T. Robinson, Martin R. West, Allyson P. Mackey, Meredith L. Rowe, John D. E. Gabrieli, 'Beyond the '30 Million Word Gap', Children's Conversational Exposure is Associated with Language-Related Brain Function. Division of Medical Sciences, Harvard University, McGovern Institute for Brain Research at the Massachusetts Institute of Technology, Department of Brain and Cognitive Sciences, Massachusetts Institute of Technology, Harvard Graduate School of Education, Department of Psychology, University of Pennsylvania.

88 Functional magnetic resonance imaging (fMRI) measures the small changes in blood flow that occur with brain activity.

89 This was independent of socio-economic status, IQ, and adult/child utterances alone.

90 The Broca's area is a region in the left hemisphere of the human brain with functions linked to speech production processing more than socioeconomic status (SES) or the quantity of words heard.

How often this happens or fails to happen in the first five years of childhood turns out to be one of the best predictors of later reading. It's almost as if a class divide exists between:

- Families that provide their children an environment rich in oral and written language opportunities.

- Families that don't.

In the above case, by kindergarten (roughly age four), a gap of 32 million words already separates some children in linguistically impoverished homes from their more stimulated peers.

What this means is that those children, who begin kindergarten having heard and used thousands of words whose meanings are already understood, classified and stored away in the brains, have the advantage in the playing field of education. Children who never have a story read to them, who never hear words that they can imagine – such as fighting dragons with a spoon or using a broom between their legs as a horse to run around in response to a story – have the odds overwhelmingly against them.

So 'lineage does matter' and parents who read to and with their children must be acknowledged!

2. When the child is reading for pleasure[91]

Contrast the above with the Adolescent Brain and Cognitive Development (ABCD) project, a US national cohort study

91 Yun-Jun Sun, Barbara J. Sahakian, Christelle Langley, Anyi Yang, Yuchao Jiang, Jujiao Kang, Xingming Zhao, Chunhe Li, Wei Cheng and Jianfeng Feng, Early-initiated childhood reading for pleasure: associations with better cognitive performance, mental well-being and brain structure in young adolescence, Cambridge University Press, 28 June 2023.

with more than 10,000 participants across different ethnicities and varying socioeconomic status. The dataset contained measures of young adolescents aged nine to 13 and how many years they had spent 'reading for pleasure' during their early childhood. It also included data on their cognitive, mental health and brain health.

There is a clear dramatic and positive link between a fun and simple activity – reading for pleasure in early childhood – and better cognition, mental health and educational attainment in adolescence.

About half of the group of adolescents started reading early in childhood, whereas the other, approximately half, had never read in early childhood, or had begun reading late on.

Researchers discovered a stunning truth:

- Reading for pleasure in early childhood was linked with better scores on comprehensive cognition assessments[92] and better educational attainment in young adolescence.

- It was also associated with fewer mental health problems and less time spent on electronic devices.

- Children who read for pleasure had larger cortical surface areas in several brain regions that are significantly related to cognition and mental health (including the frontal areas). *Importantly, this was the case regardless of socioeconomic status.*

92 The team analysed clinical interviews, cognitive tests, mental and behavioural assessments and brain scans of the 10,243 participants studied. Just under a half (48%) had little experience of reading for pleasure or did not begin doing so until later in their childhood. The remaining half had spent between three and 10 years reading for pleasure.
It then compared those who began 'reading for pleasure' between ages two and nine to those who began reading later in life, or not at all. Those who started read recreationally at an early age had better verbal learning, memory, speech development, and academic achievement than their peers who weren't picking up books for fun.

- The result therefore suggests that reading for pleasure in early childhood may be an effective intervention to counteract the negative effects of poverty on the brain.

- Therefore, it is our job to ensure that the value of intellectual skills facilitated through literacy must not be lost. The profound miracle that takes place every time a human being learns to read is one of the treasures of humanity!

Reading is a great equaliser.

Every time we hear about the *autorickshaw wallah's* son who become an IAS officer or the sweeper's son who becomes a billionaire, or India's charismatic Prime Minister Narendra Modi, who rose from *chaiwala*[93] to the highest office of the land, reading is known to unlock potential.

Modi's biographer Nikita Parmar says, *"As a young boy in hometown Vadnagar, he frequented the local library regularly, so reading has been integral to his life...Cultural heritage and ancient Indian history interest him a great deal."*

Culture is a very big deal; in that it's a defining factor in the success of individuals and teams! We must understand this in better detail. Answer this question. **"Are we smart because we read or do we read because we are smart?"**

Joe Henrich addresses this in his book, *The Secret of Our Success: How Culture Is Driving Human Evolution, Domesticating Our Species, and Making Us Smarter.* The central argument in this book is as follows:

"Relatively early in our species' evolutionary history, perhaps around the origin of our genus (Homo) about 2 million

93 Tea-stall owner.

years ago … cultural evolution became the primary driver of our species' genetic evolution. The interaction between cultural and genetic evolution generated a process that can be described as autocatalytic, meaning that it produces the fuel that propels it.

As genetic evolution improved our brains and abilities for learning from others, cultural evolution spontaneously generated more and better cultural adaptations, which kept the pressure on for brains that were better at acquiring and storing this cultural information."

It is the products of cultural evolution – such as reading – that make us smarter. We receive a huge cultural download when growing up, from a base 10 counting system, to a large vocabulary allowing us to communicate complex concepts, to the ability to read and write, not to mention the knowhow to survive. **Henrich argues that we don't have all these tools because we are smart – we are smart because we have these tools.** These cultural downloads can't be devised in a few years by a few smart people. They comprise packages of adaptations developed over generations!

CHAPTER 21

WHY READING IS MORE DIFFICULT FOR ADULTS

Let's all agree that 'learning as children' and 'learning as adults' is a little different. One way we see this is that, often, reading can feel as natural as breathing when you are a child; but sometimes, adults aren't fully able to immerse themselves in a book.

I spoke to a friend in the recruitment practice who was never a reader but had to pick it up to keep up at work. She said, *"I open my book to a page, and my eyes skim over the words; my brain doesn't comprehend them the first time. I have to re-read the words at least twice to fully soak in their meaning."* In addition, there's the pressure of responsibilities that we don't have as children! *"There are things I have to worry about now! Like getting vegetables and cooking and cleaning!" she moaned.*

When we are children, our brain and nervous system are wired[94] in all kinds of ways; like a maze. The average brain contains about 100 billion brain cells (glial cells and neurons) most of which were formed before birth. The neurons move around and are literally playing, sampling connections. This is what gives us the biological gift of *neuroplasticity* at birth; as children, we have to make almost no effort to learn!

94 Axons and dendrons

However, depending on the activities we pay attention to as we mature, particular wirings (or parts of the maze) get reinforced. The nervous system also removes connections that no longer serve it; this is a function of our experiences, travel, languages, parental environment, etc.

The other change that occurs as we mature is that in the earliest stages of childhood, new brain cells continue to be made at a brisk pace. Over the years, neurogenesis gradually declines – negligible amount of neurons get added[95] after puberty but the process doesn't stop even into older age[96].

After age 25[97], we have to work harder to make such change happen – such as reinforcing specific wirings. This is why a reading habit that's acquired in childhood is very valuable. Later in life, post 25, it takes an immense amount of focus and energy in order to learn, but that focus and energy feels almost like 'resistance.' So much so, those adults may want to back away from it, rather than fight through it.

Now this is the exact moment when you need to double down and fight this resistance[98], acknowledge it and remember that 'this is something you want to change' and reinforce it. For any cognitive skill that you want to acquire, it is important to recognise it, pay attention[99] to the resistance and push through towards the change.

Therefore, the intense backlash you're facing from yourself, the agitation, feeling overwhelmed or discomfort when you pick up a book, is not actually discomfort. It is a signal that you

95 Some evidence suggests that they get added to the olfactory senses of humans. But there's no evidence to suggested any significant addition to the memory centre.
96 However, new skills can be acquired by creating new connections between neurons.
97 Thankfully, some parts of the brain are not plastic: heartbeat, breathing, digestion etc;
98 Circulation of chemicals
99 This in itself releases the neurochemicals that help the adaptability.

are beginning the journey of learning. Your system is getting adjusted. It is also a signal that to form a new connection (reading), you have to give up an old set of connections.

Stanford scientist Andrew Huberman[100] says, *"Every activity you want to learn is telling the brain 'notice me, notice me!' There is a healthy competition going on. So whatever change you pay 'attention' to is the one that's going to win!"*

In other words, attention opens up plasticity[101]! You literally need to 'lean in' to reading or whatever it is you need to learn – cycling, swimming, driving – in order to be able to do it.

100 As explained by Andrew Huberman, Ph.D., is a neuroscientist and tenured professor in the department of neurobiology, and by courtesy, psychiatry and behavioral sciences at Stanford School of Medicine. He has made numerous significant contributions to the fields of brain development, brain function and neural plasticity, which is the ability of our nervous system to rewire and learn new behaviors, skills and cognitive functioning.
101 Multiple chemical reactions happen.

CHAPTER 22

DONE WITH COLLEGE! DO I STILL NEED TO READ?

88% of the most successful people in the world attribute their achievements to reading at least 30 minutes a day.

What are these benefits and why aren't more people reaching out for them?

Here's a theory. Everyone loves appreciation. So, behaviours **that guarantee** appreciation tend to be on full display. Perhaps, as a society, our greatest flaw is that we celebrate success in isolation; not the sweat and hard work that contributes to the success.

Beyoncé Knowles is a classic example of a glamorous singer who has based her entire 'brand' of feminism on powerful literature[102]. It is her substance that makes her, who she is, not just her stylist! But is that what we notice?

The late Charlie Munger[103] enjoyed reading just as much as his CEO Warren Buffet. Munger even made jokes about how his kids thought he was just a book with a few legs poking out since he read so much. He said famously, *"Warren and I do more reading and thinking and less doing than most people in business. We do that because we like that kind of life. But we've*

102 Beyonce routinely recommends and references *Autobiography of Malcolm X* by Malcolm X and Alex Haley, *What Will It Take To Make a Woman President?* by Marianne Schnall, *We Should All Be Feminists* by Chimamanda Ngozi Adichie and *Teaching My Mother How to Give Birth* by Warsan Shire.

103 Charlie Munger (1924-2023) is famous for being Warren Buffett's long-time business partner and the vice chairman of Berkshire Hathaway.

turned that quirk into a positive outcome for ourselves. We both insist on a lot of time being available almost every day to just sit and think. That is very uncommon in American business. We read and think."

A sustained practice of reading is well known to improve our patience and ability to consider alternatives. When we read, we hone and strengthen several different cognitive muscles, so to speak, that are the root of what we call EQ[104]. In other words, the act of reading is the very activity – if done right – develops the qualities, traits, and characteristics that give us clarity of thought.

And while we have spoken about the benefits of reading fiction, the benefits of non-fiction are considered more obvious and hence talked about more:

1. When you read, you 'collect' or 'gather' the dots... such as concepts and ideas.
2. When you follow this up with thinking about it and writing what you learnt... you 'connect' or 'link' the dots. This is explained beautifully in the work of Nobel Prize winner Eric Kandel[105].
3. Assess these dots against the reality that your life is set in. Think in a distraction-free zone. Come to your own independent learnings and conclusions.
4. Apply what you have learnt to the problems you wish to solve.

---

104 A Harvard Business Review article, 'The Case for Reading Fiction' by Christine Seifert, published in March 2020 specifically says reading fiction predicts increased social acuity and a sharper ability to comprehend other people's motivations. Reading non-fiction might certainly be valuable for collecting knowledge, it does little to develop EQ, a far more elusive goal.
105 His book, *In Search of Memory: The Emergence of a New Science of Mind* is an excellent tool to understand the basis of what we call memory.

Here's some winning advice from Mark Cuban[106],

"I read every book and magazine I could. Heck, three bucks for a magazine, 20 bucks for a book. One good idea would lead to a customer or a solution, and those magazines and books paid for themselves many times over. Some of the ideas I read were good, some not. In doing all the reading I learned a valuable lesson. ***Everything I read was public. Anyone could buy the same books and magazines. The same information was available to anyone who wanted it. Turns out most people didn't want it.***

I remember going into customer meetings or talks or go to people in the industry and tossing out tidbits about software or hardware. Features that worked, bugs in the software. All things I had read. I expected the ongoing response of: 'Oh yeah, I read that too in such-and-such.' That's not what happened. They hadn't read it then, and they still haven't starting reading it."

The benefits of reading technical material and being 'in the know' are evident. A common mistake people make is to believe that as soon as they get their jobs, the "age of studying and reading books is finally over!" The truth is quite the opposite! **Once you've finished reading what you 'have to read' in school and college, that is where reading only for your own benefit begins.** No more pressure to master subjects you don't understand. **Just read to prepare for growth.**

The owner of one of the biggest private equity funds in Singapore told me over a private conversation that *"it is very difficult to respect an employee who doesn't come prepared with thorough research for a meeting. This respect is something 'they'*

106 Mark Cuban. *How to Win at the Sport of Business: If I Can Do It, You Can Do It*, 2013.

have to earn from their seniors."

And like we have said earlier, pick any two modes of learning from the HELP matrix. But make sure to read a few pages a day to *maintain a basic cognitive level of performance.* Choose well-researched books, a mix of fiction and non-fiction and be open to recommendations outside your comfort zone!

This is especially important given that technology is adversely impacting our attention spans.[107] Since the year 2000, the average attention span of a person has dropped from 12 seconds to eight seconds. This is dropping further. Worse, much of new research and information is available exclusively online! So we don't even have a choice when it comes to checking our phones to stay updated. So how do we retain our focus?

Maybe the real question is: "will we leave a better world for our children, if we gave up reading for scrolling, or did not pass it on to them? What if they only skip and skim?"

107 A recent study led by Microsoft Canada, on the effect of technology on attention spans.

EXPERT READER ESSAY - 5

THERE'S A PART OF US THAT'S ALWAYS SEEKING TO BECOME BETTER

Let me start by saying that reading books is a terrific habit. I've been fortunate to imbibe this over a period of time. Books have always been a source of great inspiration. I must also confess that in recent days, I've been challenged. Information available via social media, mobile, internet, WhatsApp; everything is competing for attention thanks to easy accessibility.

And yet, no matter whether I've read the same information via newspapers, magazines and TV channels, reading a book gives me a different perspective. One of the books I've enjoyed recently was *Made in India* by Amitabh Kant. It offers a detailed analysis of changes that have taken place in the country with statistics, a variety of data, insightful thought processes. As I was reading it, so many thoughts came to mind. The book inspired me to see if we can understand and contribute constructively to some of the challenges that the country is taking up. It also put the spotlight on start-ups; people who have vision, direction, zeal and ideas. Such books make you realise that every Indian can become an achiever in many ways.

The behavioural benefits of reading are many; it has a massive impact on people's thought process. Books are the window to higher productivity and bring a sense of contribution to people's professional lives. We all seek to become better, get ideas and be on the path of growth and this goes up when we read books; especially about subjects such as leadership and biographies.

This book aims to inculcate the reading habit; a habit which can potentially change the life of a person. The emotional satisfaction of reading a book and the self-sufficiency provided by it can be transformative.

Imagine all of us feeling that learning is at our fingertips; and we don't always need external resources to become achievers.

Essay by Niranjan Hiranandani, *Managing Director of Hiranandani Group.*

SECTION 6

NAILING THE ARGUMENT

Solution to mind puzzle 5[108]

MIND PUZZLE 6

He was very sad. The kind of sadness that cripples you. He went out of his way to let his sadness be know. To anyone who would listen even through it would not help him at all all. Over tide, it seemed that nobody wished to peak to her anymore.

(Find all the errors in the above sentence)

108 This can end in two ways. Most of us would write something like: "Though repulsive and stinking, the sewer was vital to the drainage system in the community." Very few would go on the other track. "Though repulsive and stinking, the sewer stitched very well and people tolerated his lack of hygiene." This is how the meaning we take alters our view of what we read.

"Reading is essential for those who seek to rise above the ordinary."

– Jim Rohn[109]

109 Emanuel James Rohn, professionally known as Jim Rohn, was an American author and motivational speaker.

CHAPTER 23 READING AND PRESENCE OF MIND

The 19th century real estate developer George Addair famously said, *"Everything you've ever wanted is on the other side of fear."*

Back in the year 1999, when I was an employee at an IT firm, we were part of one of those large junkets where the Chairman of the company hobnobs with everyone else. Everyone is at their best behaviour.

That night, the affable Chairman walked around, took a moment with my colleague Anita and asked her, "So, do you think these junkets really help?" In a classic case of the spirit of the stairs[110], Anita mumbled something incoherent in front of the Chairman, only to think of a witty response a few minutes later. In a few minutes, the Chairman asked me the same question. I had no idea that he was walking around asking this question. But I responded in the most authentic way, *"Sir, I recently read 'The Six Pillars Of Self-Esteem' by Nathaniel Branden. In the book, he says that in order to grow, we have to seek discomfort. Junkets like these make us uncomfortable, because we meet so many strangers. Therefore, it is the beginning of a new journey of growth for us."*

No marks for guessing whom the Chairman remembered later.

110 Explained in Chapter 5

Reading can offer you something to say in a tricky situation. Before this job in the IT firm, during my management trainee days at Reliance Industries, I was happy to make friends with a very talented girl in the marketing department. She was senior to me, let's call her Geeta. One day, her boss came into the office open area most unexpectedly and screamed in frustration, *"Can someone give me a quick idea for this pitch?"* Now many people in the room had some vague idea but since they weren't fully sure, or couldn't remember anything specific to back it up, they kept quiet.

Geeta, however, used her reputation as a well-informed person to throw a counter-question, *"What medium are you thinking of using, sir? Outdoors or television?"*

She hadn't answered the question either!

However, when surrounded by people who didn't respond well in pressure situations and were gripped by too much fear to claim an unexpected opportunity, Geeta found her composure and triggered a discussion, to which everyone then contributed.

Mindful people (readers, meditators, etc.) are just better at navigating such moments of ambiguity. Remember that most leadership positions are all about how best to navigate ambiguity. It's not that uncertain, unexpected situations are rare. They keep showing up. And here's the real deal.

You have to assign or co-create a meaning to an ambiguous situation, be bold about the direction you're going to take and step on the gas! How does one assign or co-create meaning? By dipping into one's 'permanent information'

(which comes from reading books, among other things) and identifying the 'why' of the situation.

Sharing a few more observations from my sessions as The Reading Coach:

- If you are someone who has dropped your reading habit, you may fear picking it up again. Because **reading is difficult till it becomes easy.** And it may be intimidating. As per research from University College London[111], it may take you upto 66 days to reconnect with your habit.

- While reconnecting with your reading habit, choose a paper book rather than an e-book. Yes, reading from screens is common and will become more common in the future. And there seems to be no difference in the 'reading time' between both. However, many researchers question the effect of electronic reading on **deep reading skills, comprehension and the development of long-term knowledge and critical thinking. In other words, to reap the benefits of reading in totality, intentionally choose a paper reading experience from time to time.**

- The under-confidence that comes from not being prepared for important meetings can only be overcome by investing in self-development. While this applies to all, an important word for **business owners** and heirs to corporations: the buck stops with you! Because you work for yourself and set the standards for others!

Business leaders must make reading a part of their heir's

111 The 66-day rule is based on a study published in the European Journal of Social Psychology in 2009. Researchers at University College London conducted a study in which participants were asked to choose a new habit and track their progress for 84 days. The researchers found that it took an average of 66 days for the participants to form a new habit.

succession plans. Rishabh Mariwala, heir to the Marico fortune, recommends Simon Sinek's *Start with Why* as an important read. He took to LinkedIn to say, *"Don't skip the soul-searching"* in a long post recommending the book.

Reading can help you draw up your own language of what matters to you. You can be articulate about:

1. Whether you care about the long-term impact of your decisions.

2. Whether you have the patience to consider everyone who will get impacted.

3. Whether you can comprehend how integrity plays out in action.

4. Whether you can forget what you know and recognise outliers on their own merit? Because the real breakthroughs don't look 'normal' or 'palatable' at first.

5. Whether you can overcome your deep-rooted biases to invest in a future of innovation?

Rajiv Bajaj, who took over Bajaj Auto from his father Rahul Bajaj, famously said in an interview to the Economic Times, *"In 2008, when things started to go wrong for us, I realised that the root cause was that we didn't have the right strategy. Just a year ago, I had begun to be influenced by the work done by Al Ries and Jack Trout, two of the world's foremost strategists. When I began reading their books, at first I thought here is another Porter, heavy stuff which takes two months to finish. But when I started reading, it was wonderful."*

He credited the book *Differentiate or Die* by Jack Trout and Steve Rivkin with making a massive difference to bringing his company out of the doldrums!

CHAPTER 24 YOUR INCOME CANNOT EXCEED YOUR PERSONAL DEVELOPMENT

I wrote a poem to explain this.

A man once said to me, "If I had extra time I could make more money!"

I said, "There isn't extra time, where would you find any?
When the clock strikes 12 at midnight, the day is done!
Additional time, is available to none!"

Dejected, he started to walk away!
I said, "Wait, I do have something to say!
If making money is the point of it all!
Why don't you charge more per hour? That's all."

The man laughed, "I get paid for what I do,
How can I charge more, out of the blue?"
He was right, but I wanted to take the chance,
To make him see, even elephants can dance!

"What if you could do more?
Skills you could pick up, but have ignored!
Perhaps you could learn something new!
And then you could offer those skills too!

Your wages could be higher;
If you added more value for your hire.

Look around, who gets paid more than you?
What extra work, do they do?"

A faint glimmer of hope shone in his eyes
I'm sure he credited me with being wise!
"My boss works the same machine but manages more men!
I guess he gets paid for that then!

He does keep his wits about;
I've never seen him scream or shout!"
I said "He sounds like a good leader to me,
You can be do too, without a fancy degree!"

You can learn from anyone!
Learn quietly, post the setting sun,
Get a good mentor and two books to read.
To be fair, no one has extra time indeed!

I think the poem is self-explanatory.

What makes the difference in **'who gets paid more'** between two people is the value they bring to the table.

You can't create more time but you can become more valuable! Because you don't get paid more for your time; you get paid for your value.

CHAPTER 25 THE DELUSIONAL RISK OF SHORT-TERM LUCK

You cannot bluff or trick nature or hoodwink people beyond a point. Many people luck out in the short term and believe that they can wing it!

The problem is that the social rewards of this chance luck might get 'embedded' into your personality and delude you into thinking that you can hack life without a personal learning plan.

To understand this better, make a choice. Which one of the following are you?

A. Are you someone who has endless resources? So your mistakes have a lot of cushion.

B. Are you someone who has to optimise available resources? Your mistakes have no cushion.

Both A and B have to make sure they adopt their preferred mode of learning. We have listed all under the HELP matrix. If you are A, then you're so rich that you've gathered a bunch of sycophants around you, who will not give any 'grounded' feedback. Soon you may become B.

No matter who you are, you have to follow your own native obsession and curiosity, and decide where you want to apply your time and your intelligence and which problem you want to solve. And no matter which mode of learning you choose, reading is a great supplementary learning tool, because it will help you:

- Build some skill to earn enough to satisfy your material needs.

- Think through your own convictions.

- Decide upon a course of action for yourself.

- Find and follow your purpose.

As opposed to this, if you're going with the flow and lucking it out a few times by:

- Taking credit where it was not due to you.

- Participating in some kind of evasion or misappropriation.

- Getting lucky on a trade by guessing and believing it to be skill.

- Playing safe and counting other's losses as your success.

- Being so dependent on technology that you lack original thought.

Then, you're likely to be deluded into some notion of your own righteousness or infallibility. Trapped in such thinking, people end up pulling down corporations and even nations with their near-blind actions. They simply don't have the cognitive resources or emotional regulation to dip into, to make the right decisions. They have not strengthened their intellect with any mode of rigorous learning.

To develop fundamental clarity, Naval Ravikant often talks about two important books – *The Beginning of Infinity* and *The Fabric of Reality*. Of course, there are many more foundational books that you can choose to read. The idea is to develop your intellect and your intelligence to consider complex ideas and stay focused on your own unique creativity.

Only then can you play out the future impact of your decisions, all the way. We are going to take this a step ahead and discuss two more books by Edward Tenner. In his book, *Why Things Bite Back,* Tenner talks about 'the revenge effect.' Tenner coined this term to describe that most people aren't thinking through the technologies they employ. Technologies can solve one problem while creating additional worse problems, new types of problems, or shifting the harm elsewhere. In short, they 'bite back'.

The book, written in the 1990s, poses extremely relevant questions at a time when the world was buzzing with unbounded optimism about technology. Tenner asks:

1. Remember the Exxon Valdez oil spill? Tenner points out that 'the high-velocity hot water treatments scalded the beach and killed many organisms that had survived the original spill.' Also, the two-hundred sea otters which veterinarians rescued and sent back to sea spread a herpes virus to otters living far beyond the reach of the spill. Could this have been avoided? No, but every action or progress has unintended consequences.

2. When we introduce a new piece of technology, are we

considering whether we are interfering with a wider system? If that's the case, we should consider what might happen further down the line!

3. Does searching quickly for answers on your smartphone promote its own form of illiteracy? It would be a shame if brilliant technology were to end up threatening the brains that produced it.

Stay with these questions! Tenner is merely saying that we cannot fully anticipate all dimensions of the outcomes of technological progress.

In his other book, *The Efficiency Paradox: What Big Data Can't Do,* Tenner says, "Trying to be ultimately efficient at all times will succeed in the short run," he says. "But in the long run, you would be damaging your efficiency."

Tenner advises us to use common sense and balance things out – take full advantage of being human – instead of trapping ourselves by opting for just one way to do things.

He says, ***"There are many things that even little children can appreciate that the most advanced technologies of machine learning can't, and I think that to me is one of the most exciting things about the mind and about being human. One example is how little children can understand the meaning of a proverb – like "a stitch in time saves nine" or "a rolling stone gathers no moss" – in a way that a computer can't… Don't be afraid of your common sense."***

Borrowing a leaf from these greats, I'd like to add:

- Feeling smart after getting your answers from a Google search followed by a headline scroll may be a lot like enhancing your features with cosmetic surgery! It's simply not real and sooner or later all implants will give into gravity (which is real, by the way) and start sagging!

- Falling prey to the 'high dopamine digital culture', repeatedly, is like keeping a tiger in a cage and making it lazy by feeding it with meat purchased from the market! After a while, if you expect it to go hunting, it will resist! The tiger has lost the art of 'being a tiger!' Once you're used to the easier life, it's extremely difficult to retrain yourself to work hard again. So find the time to add a healthy dose of analogue print reading in your day. It will compound over time to unimaginable benefits.

- Being in denial about the **loss of skills due to lack of reading** will not help. We were in denial about climate change too! The problem didn't go away because we didn't acknowledge it.

- It's tragic that brands are constantly asking advertising agencies to appeal to people's diminishing attention spans all the time. Their mandate is to 'engage' people's attention with 'sparkly', 'click-bait' content, which skims the surface with sensational headlines. Protect the permanent information; be the gatekeeper of the reading habit for your family, your friends and larger community.

Remember that reading is truly magical and miraculous.

1. We invented reading: Deep reading is our species' 'bridge' into insight and novel, original thought.

2. We apply background knowledge to new information, seek parallels, draw conclusions, apply logic, check for falsehoods

and also learn a new perspective, expanding our empathy and knowledge. This is much like critical analysis. By contrast, when we skim, we physiologically jump over all these deeper processes.

3. The specifics of this activity matter. Serious reading is an exceptional activity. We must prioritise this to live a deep life.

4. Random Google search has its uses but it is not to be confused with research. Go to a real library (online or offline) and see how real researchers index their studies and how many layers and caveats there are to each study. And how humble they are when they admit that 'they do not have the answers.' Do the deep work.

5. Avoiding focused work of some kind is like avoiding walking. Sure, you can sit around but it's not a healthy choice in the long run. The same applies to older children and adults.

Think about it. The days when you fall ill, you'll find it extremely difficult to read a book. But you can still scroll the internet or watch a movie. Because hard choices easy life, easy choices hard life!

To get the body you want, you have to do the exercise you need, not the one that's easy. To compound the value of your work, you want to play long-term games with long-term people. To be able to access the deepest recesses of the capacity of your brain and your imagination, you have to read the good books!

Like Aristotle said, "the ability to think deeply" is the essence of being human.

CHAPTER 26

A READING CHECKLIST FOR THE POTENTIAL CEO

Here are 40 books for those who aspire to be CEO before they turn 40.

Remember to tweak these as per:
- Your hobbies and personal choices
- The language you prefer to read in. Reading in any language has the same decagonal benefits!

1. *An Intimate Note to the Sincere Seeker* by Gurudev Sri Sri Ravi Shankar
2. *Proust and the Squid* by Maryanne Wolf
3. *The Logic of Failure: Recognising and Avoiding Error in Complex Situations* by Dietrich Dörner translated by Rita and Robert Kilmer
4. *Journey to Ixtlan: The Lessons of Don Juan* by Carlos Castaneda
5. *How Big Things Get Done* by Bent Flyvbjerg
6. *Meditations* by Marcus Aurelius
7. *Essentialism: The Disciplined Pursuit of Less* by Greg McKeown.
8. *The Forgotten Highlander: My Incredible Story of Survival During the War in the Far East* by Alistair Urquhart
9. *Change Your Thoughts, Change Your Life* by Dr. Wayne Dyer

10. *Autobiography of a Yogi* by Paramahansa Yogananda
11. *Lying* by Sam Harris
12. *The Ape that Understood the Universe* by Steve Stewart Williams
13. *The Precipice* by Toby Old
14. *Lost Connections* by Yohann Hari
15. *Freedom from the Known* by Jiddu Krishnamurthy
16. *The War of Art* by Steven Pressfield
17. *Endurance* by Alfred Lansing
18. *Why We Sleep* by Matthew Walker
19. *Anti-fragile* by Nassim Nicholas Taleb
20. *The Prince* by Niccolo Machiavelli
21. *Longitude* by Dave Sobel
22. *The Gentleman in Moscow* by Amor Knowles
23. *Behind the Beautiful Forevers: Life, Death and Hope in a Mumbai Undercity* by Katherine Boo
24. *On the Origin of Species* by Charles Darwin
25. *The Effective Executive* by Peter Drucker
26. *Awareness* by Anthony DMello
27. *Little, Big: or, The Fairies' Parliament* by John Crowley
28. *Thinking, Fast and Slow* by Daniel Kahneman
29. *The Most Important Thing* by Howard Marks
30. *The Power of Now* by Eckhart Tolle
31. *The History of Strategy* by Lawrence Friedman
32. *Sea of Poppies* by Amitav Ghosh
33. *Crime and Punishment* by Fyodor Dostoevsky
34. *A History of Reading* by Alberto Manguel
35. *The Rights of Man* by Thomas Paine
36. *1984* by George Orwell

37. *Faust* by Johann Wolfgang von Goethe
38. *Getting to Yes* by William Ury and Roger Fisher
39. *Loonshots* by Safi Bahcall
40. *Big Sister, Little Sister, Red Sister: Three Women at the Heart of Twentieth-Century China* by Jung Chang.

CHAPTER 27

READING JUST SIX MINUTES PER DAY!

During my sessions as The Reading Coach, I advise people to reconnect with reading by starting with six minutes per day!

This is based on research carried out by Mindlab International at the University of Sussex which says that **reading for only six minutes reduces stress levels by 68%, making it more effective than listening to music (61%), having a cuppa[112] (54%), taking a walk (42%), or playing video games (21%).**

Researchers believe that the concentration required for reading has a physiological effect on the brain, contributing to a shutdown of the emergency fight or flight response. As the stress hormones dissipate, the 'fear centre of the brain becomes less active' and the rationalisation areas of the brain take over.

Given these benefits, I was keen to suggest a base 'entry level' routine, by which it might be possible for all of us to make these six minutes a habit. And the reason why these six minutes should be a physical book, is because there are two main kinds of reading: linear and non-linear.

112 warm beverage such as tea or coffee

• Linear reading: The reader reads the text from the left to the right start to finish. Also known as slow reading or deep reading. This is paper reading.

• Non-linear reading: The reader skims material jumping to different sections. Also known as scattered reading, which causes a sensory fatigue. This is digital reading.

Reading physical material is all about attention. For example, along with reading,

1. You cannot drive a car
2. You cannot put clothes into the washing machine
3. You cannot cook.
4. Basically, there's no other activity you can do alongside reading.

When you're reading online, the entire environment is different. Distractions are built into the environment itself. We have said before that screen reading scores low on the **priming effect**[113]. The manner and psychological makeup with which we approach the internet itself is different from how we approach physical reading. For one, it's the ease itself of scrolling and clicking. This reduces the 'rigour' of the activity somewhat. With a lower demand being placed on the mental faculties, the online environment is far less 'serious.' More often than not, attractive-looking links lead to unrelated material and they're quite tempting. Before you know it, the two-minute search becomes a 20-minute distraction. This is way less effective!

Six minutes on digital devices therefore won't cut it! You are better off picking up a physical book.

113 The priming effect is a cognitive bias: it describes how exposure to a stimulus can influence a person's response to a subsequent stimulus without conscious intent.

The next question is, how many days before this becomes a habit? There are many debates on this. There is compelling evidence that 66[114] days may just be the right duration. This timeframe may be particularly relevant for work habits, which often involve complex and multifaceted behaviours that require consistent effort and practice to become ingrained.

To all the people who have been part of The Reading Coach training program and heard me say, start reading six minutes a day for 66 days, this is a suggestion. There is no one-size-fits-all approach to developing new habits. You may need less[115] or more than 66 days to succeed at this! The key is to focus on small, sustainable changes and stay committed to the process of growth and improvement over time.

Interestingly, there's evidence to suggest that 'reading aloud' was the norm in the 3rd century.

1. The need to constantly block other kinds of notifications leads to shallower processing of the information.
2. Constant exposure to blue light from screens can be hard on the eyes over time. Thanks to advanced technology, most screens flicker (far outside the human range these days) in an almost imperceptible manner. Yet, this could potentially cause sensory fatigue.

114 Refer page 116

115 Phillippa Lally, a health psychology researcher at University College London published a study in the European Journal of Social Psychology about the duration for habit formation. Lally and her research team examined the habits of 96 people over a 12-week period. Each person chose one new habit for the 12 weeks and reported each day on whether or not they stuck to the task and how automatic the task felt. For example, 'drinking a bottle of water with lunch' or 'running for 15 minutes before dinner.' After 12 weeks, the researchers analysed the data to determine how long it took each person to go from starting a new behaviour to automatically doing it. On an average, it took more than two months before the new behaviour became automatic – 66 days to be exact. However, the range in Lally's study is extremely important; it took anywhere from 18 days to 254 days for people to form a new habit.

CHAPTER 28 THE PERILS OF DIGITAL-ONLY READING

This chapter is a reiteration of what we have learnt so far with some fresh perspectives.

We are simply not going to be able to avoid digital reading! One of the reasons we have all adopted digital reading is 'convenience' and 'efficiency.' It's so much faster to read off the phone when you're in an emergency. All I am saying is:

- From time to time, read off physical print.

- Be aware of the unintended consequences of digital-only reading.

The important question is how is the shift from paper reading to digital reading transforming our brain itself?

We don't fully know yet!

Author Maryanne Wolf says that our brain's neuroplasticity is the biggest risk we are facing. And we are not going to be able to control this!

"The act of going beyond the text to analyse, infer and think new thoughts is the product of years of formation. It takes time, both in milliseconds and years, and effort to learn to read with deep, expanding comprehension and to execute all these processes as an adult expert reader.

When it comes to building this reading circuit in a brain that has no preprogrammed setup for it, there is no genetic guarantee that any individual novice reader will ever form the expert reading brain circuitry that most of us form."

I'm going to reiterate this in a different way! Future generations that never learn to read from print in a linear fashion may not develop the skills we take for granted today.

One of the architects of our nation, legendary banker Deepak Parekh of HDFC famously says that throughout his career, he devoured printed newspapers for a few hours every day!

Wolf adds, *"The reading circuit's very plasticity is also its Achilles' heel. It can be fully fashioned over time and fully implemented when we read, or it can be short-circuited – either early on in its formation period or later, after its formation, in the execution of only part of its potentially available cognitive resources."*

This short circuiting of cognitive resources is dangerous because it implies a sub-optimal development of our brains. Patricia Marks Greenfield, researcher in the field of human development explains, "Every medium has its costs and weaknesses; every medium develops some cognitive skills at the expense of others...the Internet may develop impressive visual intelligence, the cost seems to be to deep processing: mindful knowledge acquisition, inductive analysis, critical thinking, imagination and reflection." So, our brain is evolving or devolving all over again. Are we going to lose the decagonal benefits we have painstakingly gained and passed down?

The answer seems to be yes!

In the words of Tristan Harris, **"Digital designers use same addiction-producing design principles as casinos, just as the tobacco industry knowingly used nicotine to addict without telling the public."**

This is simply unhealthy. The brain's neuroplasticity will ensure that it adapts in a different direction, basis the new inputs that it is receiving.

This brings me to a very sad but important quote by Stephen Jay Gould[116]:

"I am somehow less interested in the weight and convolutions of Einstein's brain than in the near certainty that people of equal talent have lived and died in cotton fields and sweatshops!"

Often, perfectly capable minds have never been able to experience the benefits of the full capacity of their cognitive prowess! They fall prey to 'addiction' over 'attention' and that path is a downward spiral.

Are we at a tipping point, about to waste generations of intelligence? Will further research prove otherwise?

116 Stephen Jay Gould was a 20th century American paleontologist, evolutionary biologist, and historian of science.

CHAPTER 29 SOCIAL MEDIA FOR ITS OWN SAKE, PLEASE

I use social media to talk about the benefits of reading! Paradoxical?

Maybe not. Because I am a digital *PLUS* physical reader as most millennials are. One by dint of necessity and the other by choice. Digital reading is how we deal with work emails and WhatsApp. It is also part of writing this manuscript on my laptop right now.

But social media is distinct from this. It is a great tool for professional networking; you can put your work and identity out there. It also diminishes the distance between you and your idols, bringing their thought process closer to you than ever before. Think of Naval Ravikant's famous tweet storm for instance. I also enjoyed listening to the Joe Rogan podcast with Elon Musk. But remember that these are informative and application-oriented but not application-ready. When I have to apply something, I have to dig in deeper.

Unfortunately, social media is full of non-informative stuff too. Six out of 10 youngsters in India in the 9-17 age group spend over three hours daily on various social media. Almost 17% of the respondents added that their kids were on social media for more than six hours a day. This is where it becomes unhealthy!

Since young children don't have the maturity to differentiate between useful and non-useful applications of technology, social media seems to be taking 'play-time' away and giving our kids anxiety, depression, headaches and neck and back pain due to poor posture!

On the subject of 'play' a new book *The Anxious Generation* by Jonathan Haidt talks about the benefits of free play that we all indulged in as kids. **Haidt says that the small challenges and setbacks that happen during 'play' are like an inoculation that prepares children to face much larger challenges later! He laments how free play began to decline in the 1980s. This decline accelerated in the 90s. Hereafter, the rapid spread of high-speed broadband in the 2000s, arrival of the iPhone in 2007 and the like and retweet buttons that appeared in 2009, meant that the life of Gen Z would never be the same again!**

The author also points out that a phone-based life often fills 'our life's search for meaning' with trivial and degrading content! As opposed to meaningful content from good books maybe? Or any form of deep work?

A study by the American Journal of Preventive Medicine[117] featured 1,787 U.S. adult participants aged 19–32 years using a sampling frame that represented 97% of the U.S. population. Those in the top 25% of social media usage had twice the odds of having greater perceived social isolation.

"Higher the social media usage, more the perceived social isolation."

117 Social Media Use and Perceived Social Isolation Among Young Adults in the U.S. Brian A. Primack, MD, PhD et al, VOLUME 53, ISSUE 1, P1-8, JULY 2017.

Another study by Dr. Jean Twenge[118], professor of psychology at San Diego State University, in 2020 suggests that 'there is an increase in depression, self-harm, and suicide cases among American young adults due to the increase in technology use'. Constant usage of social media for short periods of time, like waiting in a queue at the grocery market, makes us completely dependent, thus adding to our already shortened attention span.

We are reaching out unconsciously to our phones. We cannot bear a minute with ourselves, or so it seems!

Social media is not the only misused aspect of technology. Technology enables people to multitask. You can do various things at once, just by sitting or standing in one place.

I distinctly remember a case when a young trader was standing in front of me and half talking to me, half chatting with his friend trying to rescue a cat, half scrolling moneycontrol.com with one eye on his trading monitor. He entered a buy on 10,000 shares instead of 1,000 shares! Imagine the fallacy of believing that you have it all together between five distinct activities!

Multi-tasking, even though it has been projected as advantageous, decreases our attention span! You're more likely to make mistakes because distractions and switching between tasks tires out the brain. You'll also remember way lesser, as the information doesn't get encoded properly into long-term memory.

118 She has authored the brilliant book *'Igen: Why Today's Super-Connected Kids Are Growing Up Less Rebellious, More Tolerant, Less Happy--and Completely Unprepared for Adulthood--and What That Means for the Rest of Us'*

Multitasking reduces our brain to a fraction of its ability to focus; we end up 'blaming luck when we lose' and 'credit our skill when we win', constantly fooled by the randomness of it all!

Many successful people mindfully stay away from scrolling. Because life's grand adventures unfold offline. Ever done a Mount Everest trek or visited the Kumbh Mela?

Elon Musk, who owns social media company X among other things, says, *"A lot of social media is bad for kids, as there is extreme competition between social media AIs to maximise dopamine!"* Balance is critical. The brilliance of the human brain, which created the technologies we enjoy, must not be dimmed by it.

There seems to be a sliver of hope! Australia has banned social media for kids under 16.

In India, the Digital Personal Data Protection Act, which was passed into law in August, has proposed age-gating.

This might be a big saviour for future generations, if we are able to explain it well to our children. Social media will have to conduct some form of age-verification of children – that is, users below the age of 18 – through documents stored either in DigiLocker, an Aadhaar-based process, a digital token, or at the app store level, depending on the risk of a child's data being possibly misused and the likely harm!

What do you think of this?

EXPERT READER ESSAY - 6

READING ENHANCES ALL OTHER LIFE EXPERIENCES

Reading is essential to most vocations, including journalism. For one, you have to be aware of your professional environment. Reading also anchors you in your own reality. This is fundamental to crafting your identity and the value you bring to your work.

I have had the privilege of training hundreds of young journalists in my lifetime. In fact, my cabin was always full of books and I would give of them freely. One of the most surprising things to me as an Editor-in-Chief over the years has been that there are many journalists who don't read. Not even their own newspapers! I have repeatedly said, *"There are things I can teach you about writing; but you will not understand the nuances till you have read a vast range of writers.'*

I particularly remember this very bright intern. All of 19, she was naturally blessed with a very good flair for language. She looked up to me in a very sincere way and was keen to improve her craft. We shared a wonderful mentee-mentor relationship and I could see how her turn of phrase, metaphors and sentence structure improved with reading! She applied herself creditably and read in a focused manner to improve her work. This kind of functional attitude to reading is creditable too! The only kind of attitude I detest is *"where is the time to read!"* *or worse still, "reading is a waste of time!"*

The other approach to books that surprises me is that the minute you ask a seasoned reader for book recommendations, they rattle off a list of only self-help books! For sure, I have read Dale Carnegie, *Ikigai* and Marie Kondo and found them useful. But that's not all there is to books. Fiction is such an imaginative experience. I am reading Margaret Atwood's *Oryx and Crake* and I cannot begin to describe the journey it is taking me on! I have found joy in Murakami and Neil Gaiman, in equal measure.

While it is true that reading non-fiction has its advantages, we need to actively recommend fiction as well. The one thing I'm not such a big fan of are biographies; they are often economical with the truth[119]!

No matter what you're reading, it is an active process! You create all kinds of scenes in your mind! Reading is like osmosis, you absorb, reflect and pause as you consider your own point of view. In contrast, watching a movie is passive because you're being spoon-fed the entire scene.

Thankfully, watching movies and reading books need not be mutually exclusive, so one can enjoy both. I can like both cooking and gardening! It is possible to have and sustain more than one interest! Books are also great conversation starters! And yes, there is something to be said for the quality of books itself.

The quality of what you read is so important that I once told my daughter *"no more young adult fiction! Can you move to something more cerebral?"*

I also believe that Book Clubs have a massive role to play in maintaining thriving communities that read; I was part of one such called Book Masala in Bengaluru. They cement the realisation that reading is not a coldly analytical experience but a warm, immersive and collaborative experience.

119 Being a committed biographer, the author of this book – yours truly – wanted to delete this sentence.

And yes, while it is true that there are many ways to learn, reading is sure to:

- Enhance your travel experience

- Uplift your spiritual journey

- Give you the tools to pursue your passion

What more can you ask for?

Essay by Purba Dutt, *veteran Times of India journalist.*

SECTION 7

TOOLS AND TECHNIQUES

Solution to mind puzzle 6[120]

120 He was very sad. The kind of sadness that cripples you. He went out of his way to let his sadness be know (add n here). To anyone who would listen even through (though) it would not help him at all all (all is repeated). Over tide (this should be time) it seemed that nobody wished to peak (speak) to her (the gender has changed) anymore.
We make many adjustments as we read, in order to read better. This is because reading is a highly nuanced skill!

"Think before you speak. Read before you think."

– Fran Lebowitz [121]

121 Fran Lebowitz is a celebrated comedienne and author of numerous books, including *Metropolitan Life*

CHAPTER 30 FINDING FOCUS IN THE AGE OF INTERRUPTION

So, we are in 'the Age of Interruption.' Some may say, also in the age of overload.

We live in a time that is often called 'the Age of Information', a time when we are surrounded by seemingly endless repositories of data. Writing in 1997, journalist Jennifer Tanaka[122] observed that, *"A single weekday edition of The New York Times today contains more information than an average person in the 17th century would have encountered in a lifetime. Over a decade later, the information to which we are exposed on a daily basis has increased exponentially, and most of it now resides on the Internet."*

Since Tanaka's times, this has only grown exponentially! But the Internet brings us more than information. **With the advent of high-speed transmission, mobile devices, and Web 2.0, it also offers the possibility of constant connectivity, which means that the Internet is extremely useful. There's nothing wrong with it, except in our use of it! We need to shift the blame elsewhere; maybe to ourselves?**

And once we accept our role in the declining attention spans and other perils, we can perhaps reconnect to reading. Here

122 Jennifer Tanaka, "Drowning in Data," Newsweek, 4/28/98, p. 85

are a few mindful tips to begin your reading journey:

1. Books are transformative, but only if we take action upon what we've learned: If you want to make a career jump from say marketing to journalism, you have to read books on how to become a better writer. The action lesson is an important one. We have the power to let our favourite books change our lives through action.

2. Make your reading 'social': Reading is most valuable when we share what we're reading and learning with others. Joining book clubs and attending author signings, for example, help you connect with others around a love of books. Talking about the lessons from books helps it settle in more deeply in our consciousness, and gaining outside perspective creates adjustments and illuminations around what we read that we would otherwise miss.

3. Choose what you like: With so many books vying for attention, choosing what to read next can feel overwhelming. But reading what you like is key to sustain the habit. Timing is everything; choose books that resonate with you, wherever you are in life at that point! Does the book tell a story on a topic you're curious about? Does the book solve a problem you're facing? Connect the dots is an interesting strategy – if an author lights you up, check out their other work. Or research that author, and see if you can discover what books influenced them the most.

4. Don't be critical of your choices: New readers often feel that "their reading habits are poor." They feel almost embarrassed about their reading choices. The truth is, you're free to read anything you want. Reading is personal. The more personal it is, the more powerful it gets. Reading is active – so read for the present moment. Think of reading like a conversation with the author. Challenge what the author is telling you. Take notes and make highlights, so your ideas and insights are preserved; mull over them. This is how we foster creativity and form our own unique insights. Active reading is a superpower.

5. Take ownership of your personal development: Study the HELP matrix. Choose reading to layer on the two practices you will follow. Remember that you have access to the most invaluable pieces of information and knowledge in the form of books. Bill Gates wrote a book on climate change, *How To Avoid a Climate Disaster*, have you read it? He has access to information and conversations at levels that you and I don't. Why would we ignore what he has to say? Get informed about the world we are living in so that your actions become more meaningful.

6. Form a bookshelf of mentors: Imagine you're hiring three life coaches:

a. Rafael Nadal (never give up)

b. Sam Walton (how to build a big business)

c. Abraham Lincoln (for how to handle your rivals)

Which area of your life do you need mentoring in? Obviously, none of us may be able to meet them one on one (even if they were alive!). **But having a bookshelf of mentors depending on the skill sets you want to build is one of the most cost-effective routes to personal development.**

7. Form a pre-reading ritual: Set an agenda/purpose for why you're reading a particular book. It puts you in a very determined state of mind. For example, if you want to lose weight, then that's what you should read about. Next, find the books that will help you. Once you shortlist say five books, check which of the authors is most appealing to you by reading up about them, checking out the book reviews or watching a video of them speaking. Lastly, commit to reading the book. While reading, have a dedicated place, mug, desk, and notepad, Post-Its, etc. Make notes when you learn something important that you might like to come back to. Make sure you write in a way that you will be able to identify readily.

8. Remember to keep science books on your reading list: Scientists never assume; they may be on the verge of an important discovery but they will still not declare anything till it's proven. This is a lesson in humility, gratitude and foundational knowledge. Reading about scientific progress connects us to the journey we have made as humankind itself. Here's a science book checklist for you.

- *Foundation* series by Isaac Asimov: This is an epic saga of a mathematician's efforts to preserve knowledge and steer humanity's future.

- *The Moon Is a Harsh Mistress* by Robert Heinlein: The tale of a lunar colony's struggle for independence.

- *Structures: Or Why Things Don't Fall Down* by J.E. Gordon: The book serves as a primer on the intricacies of structural stability and engineering prowess.

- *Einstein: His Life and Universe* by Walter Isaacson: The book offers a deep dive into the life and mind of one of history's greatest thinkers who pursued groundbreaking ideas.

9. Always carry a book: This is extremely important. We wait everywhere; in airports, for appointments and even when we have nothing better to do in a traffic jam. We definitely wait more than six minutes a day in some situation or another. Keep a thin book always handy so that you don't lose your patience to the situation.

10. Never feel guilty about not completing a book: Read Chapter 10 again! **The way we read changes as we go through life, and reading changes the life we go through.**

CHAPTER 31

EXPERT Q&As

Readers are a spectrum by themselves. We all have been readers through our education, focusing on academic reading. Some of us grow into mindful readers who read optimally, reaching out for a book when we have a problem to solve. There are those who consume novels for pleasure. There are avid readers who are committed to reading all kinds of books to understand the world better. There are history lovers; those who stock large libraries and refer to books out of nostalgia and finally those that are teetering on the fringes – to read or not to read?

In this chapter, we speak to a couple of avid readers and ask them for book recommendations.

A. Sasha Mirchandani of Kae Capital

1. Can you recollect a time when a book made you reconsider a decision?

***The Alchemist* by Paulo Coelho.** *This novel led me to reconsider my life goals and dreams. It has inspired me to pursue my passions and to trust in my journey of life.*

2. Tell me about a book that gave you a whole new perspective.

***Thinking, Fast and Slow* by Daniel Kahneman.** *This book* *has changed how I understand human decision-making and cognitive biases. It provides insights into the two systems of thought that govern our decisions and highlights the irrationality inherent in human thinking.*

3. Did you enjoy reading a book that's not really considered a traditional bestseller? Something you discovered and warmed your heart?

I have enjoyed reading the book, ***The Ultimate Gift*** **by Jim Stovall.** *Each 'gift' in the book is not just a narrative but also a piece of practical wisdom. I appreciated the actionable advice and the way it encouraged me to apply these lessons to my own life.*

B. Hemant Amin, Asiamin family office. He counts the great Charlie Munger as one of his personal mentors. We asked him for three recommendations for today's youth!
"Reading is fundamental to learning. I strongly recommend the following books to people of all ages."

1. *Poor Charlie's Almanac* by Charlie Munger

This book offers incredible insights into mental models, decision-making, and how to succeed in both business and personal life. It provides a thoughtful approach to life and relationships, making it a must-read for anyone interested in developing practical wisdom.

2. *Rich Dad Poor Dad* by Robert Kiyosaki

It is a classic for learning the basics of financial literacy and understanding our relationship with money. It teaches the importance of financial independence and how to shift one's mindset to build long-term wealth rather than living paycheck to paycheck.

3. *Meditations* by Marcus Aurelius

A great introduction to stoicism, this book helps bring balance and purpose to life. It encourages readers to focus on what they can control and develop emotional resilience, skills that are invaluable in today's fast-paced and often stressful world.

These three books cover essential aspects of life – critical thinking, financial management, and emotional balance – making them ideal reads for young people today.

CHAPTER 32 THE 'WHAT SHOULD I READ' QUESTIONNAIRE

As a Reading Coach, *I am extremely keen to engage with you. For a personal book recommendation for free, fill in this questionnaire and email to reeta@reetaramamurthygupta.in*

Section 1: Hobbies and Interests

1. What are your main hobbies and interests outside of reading?
2. How do these hobbies influence your choice of reading material?
3. Do you prefer reading books related to your hobbies? If so, can you provide examples?
4. Are there any hobbies or interests you wish you had more time to explore through reading?

Section 2: Parental Influence

5. How did your parents or guardians influence your reading habits when you were growing up?
6. Were you encouraged to read from a young age? If yes, how?
7. Did your parents read to you or with you? If so, what kinds of books were read?
8. How did your family's attitude towards reading affect your

own reading habits?

Section 3: Financial Background

9. What was your family's financial situation like when you were a child?
10. Did your financial situation affect the number of books you had access to as a child? If yes, how?
11. Were you ever involved in book exchanges, libraries, or book fairs during your childhood?
12. How did your financial background impact your ability to buy or access books as a child?

Section 4: Extent of Reading

13. How many books do you read on average per month?
14. What types of books do you read most often (e.g., fiction, non-fiction, genres)?
15. Do you set reading goals or challenges for yourself? If so, what are they?
16. How do you track or manage your reading (e.g., reading logs, apps, journals)?

Section 5: Depth of Reading

17. Do you prefer to read books in-depth (e.g., analysing themes, characters) or more casually?
18. Are there specific genres or subjects you dive deeply into?
19. How often do you revisit books you've read before?
20. Do you engage in discussions or book clubs related to your reading? If so, how frequently?

Section 6: Role Models and Influences

21. Who are your literary role models or authors that have influenced your reading habits?

22. Have any public figures or celebrities influenced your choice of reading material? If so, who?
23. Do you follow any particular book critics or reviewers? How do they affect your reading choices?
24. How have your friends or social circles influenced your reading habits?

Section 7: Reflection and Future Reading

25. Looking ahead, are there any specific genres, authors, or types of books you plan to explore or learn more about?

Feel free to adjust or expand any questions based on your specific needs or interests!

QR code for The Reading Coach website

CHAPTER 33

THE 'WHY AM I NOT READING' QUESTIONNAIRE

Are you someone who gave up reading over time but doesn't know why? Are you someone who has never read but are convinced that it can help you? Fill in this questionnaire and email to reeta@reetaramamurthygupta.in to check on how you can become a reader again.

Section 1: General Attitudes Towards Reading

1. How do you define reading?
2. What are your general thoughts or feelings about reading?
3. Can you describe any experiences that led you to believe that reading is a waste of time?
4. Do you believe that reading can be beneficial in any way? Why or why not?
5. How do you feel when you see other people engaged in reading?

Section 2: Childhood Experiences

6. What was your early exposure to books and reading like?
7. Were books and reading emphasised in your household growing up? If so, how?
8. Did you have access to books as a child? What kinds of books were available to you?
9. Did you participate in reading-related activities, such as library visits or book clubs, as a child?

10. Can you recall any negative experiences with books or reading during your childhood?

Section 3: Family and Social Influences

11. How did your family members view reading and books?
12. Were there any role models in your family who were avid readers? How did their habits influence you?
13. Did your friends or peers show interest in reading? How did their attitudes affect you?
14. Were there any social pressures or expectations related to reading when you were growing up?

Section 4: Educational Impact

15. How was reading incorporated into your schooling?
16. Did you find any aspect of your educational experience related to reading challenging or unenjoyable?
17. Were there any particular books or texts from school that you found particularly uninteresting or difficult?
18. Did you receive any encouragement or discouragement related to reading from teachers or mentors?

Section 5: Personal Interests and Alternatives

19. What are your primary interests or hobbies?
20. How do you spend your leisure time, and why do you prefer these activities over reading?
21. Have you ever tried to read books related to your interests or hobbies? What was your experience?
22. Are there any other activities or forms of media you find more engaging than reading? Why?

Section 6: Perceived Value and Benefits

23. What do you think are the benefits of reading, if any?

24. Why do you believe these benefits do not apply to you personally?
25. Do you think reading could have any impact on your personal or professional life? If not, why?

Section 7: Biases and Misconceptions
26. Do you think there are any misconceptions or biases you hold about reading? What are they?
27. Where do you think these biases originated?
28. Have you encountered any stereotypes or negative portrayals of readers or reading that might have influenced your views?
29. Are there any specific genres or types of books you've avoided? Why?

Section 8: Potential Triggers for Change
30. What would need to change for you to consider reading as a valuable activity?
31. Are there specific situations or contexts that might make you more open to reading?
32. Would you be willing to try reading under different circumstances (e.g., a book recommended by a trusted friend)?

Section 9: Personal Reflections
33. How do you feel about your current reading habits, or lack thereof?
34. Do you think your views on reading might change in the future? What could influence that change?
35. What role do you think reading plays in personal development and growth?
36. How do you think society's view on reading affects your own perspective?

Section 10: Evaluating Past Experiences

37. Have you had any significant life experiences that have influenced your views on reading?
38. Did you have any memorable experiences with books or reading that were particularly positive or negative?
39. How do these past experiences compare with your current views on reading?

Section 11: Final Thoughts

40. Is there anything else you would like to share about your views on reading?
41. Do you have any suggestions for how reading could be made more appealing or relevant to people with your perspective?
42. Would you be interested in discussing your views on reading with others who have different perspectives?

QR code for The Reading Coach website

CHAPTER 34

FUNNILY ENOUGH, AI ENGINEERS ARE TELLING US HOW POWERFUL THE READING BRAIN IS

This chapter has to be the last word! The sheer capability of the human brain is not as evident to anyone as much as it is to AI developers. They feel stuck because:

1. It is not easy to correlate brain capability with the specific area responsible for it.

2. The human brain was not designed from scratch. There was no initial blueprint which had to be followed. It just kept evolving over time in a long sequence of steps. The knowledge and functionality of one step is key to understanding the next step.

Roughly speaking, this chart is the closest to understanding the various functions and areas of the brain, as they developed.

	Neurons	Function
Early Eumetazoans (eg coral polyps)	Nerve nets	Sensile nature, wait for food to come, respond when food comes.
Early bilaterians	Valence neurons, first brain	Reward, associative learning, affective states
Early vertebrates	Forebrain, midbrain, hindbrain, basal ganglia	Interval timing, pattern recognition, trial and error, spatial mapping
Early mammals	Neocortex	Consider options before acting (superior to trial and error), counterfactual learning, episodic memory
Early primates	Granular pre-frontal cortex, motor cortex connection	Theory of mind, imitation learning, anticipating future needs
Early humans	Frontal development, motor cortex connects to larynx.	Language, beat based timing

This is how we know for sure that learning was not the core function of the first ever brain that appeared in a multicellular body.

Suggested steps of brain evolution.

STEP 1

The purpose of the first brain was to taxi – move towards or away from something. Roughly 600 million years ago, we had nerve nets in the brain. This meant that even without eyes and ears, organisms such as nematodes could find food. There is activity without sensory input to help the body steer towards good and away from bad.

STEP 2

The purpose of the early vertebrate brain (for example, fish) is much more developed. Sensory input appeared. We also see that behaviour is optimised for reward, viz. fish would recognis patterns and engage in trial and error basis the patterns.

STEP 3

This is the phase where the early mammal brain learnt by imagining, thanks to the neocortex. What this means is to recognise patterns and consider options BEFORE trial and error. Episodic memory emerged – the ability to recall past events and use these to adjust behaviour. The motor cortex also evolved, allowing vertebrates to plan movement better.

STEP 4

The first primate brain was much more evolved. The neocortex developed even further in the following ways.

- Could accept different interpretations of the world
- Could imitate each other and learn

- Make a decision now by anticipating a need in the future

They could essentially 'mentalize' (understand intent).

STEP 5

We have finally reached the first human brain. We learnt to SPEAK! Thanks to the gift of language, ideas could now be perpetuated down generations! The brain became bigger and cooking emerged to give the brain the energy to grow larger! The brain over time also learned to read and write, resulting in unprecedented progress!

As per Max Bennet, who wrote the book A *Brief History of Intelligence,* the pyramid of development of the human brain over time is as follows.

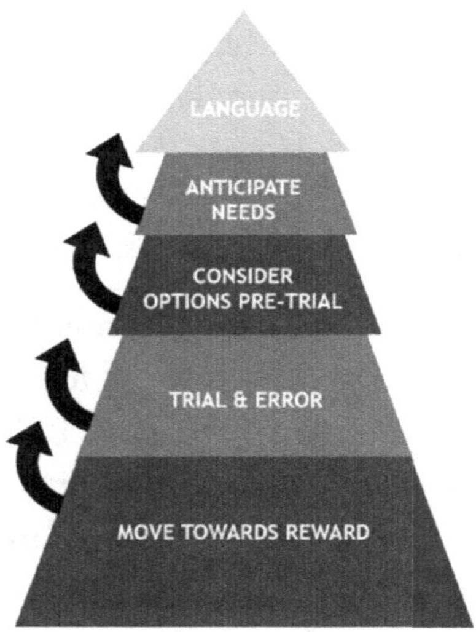

Picture 6 : The Brain Pyramid

It seems difficult to believe that reading came to us only in the last 15% of our own evolution; even though it's an essential part of our daily lives today.

"Those who don't read are in danger of becoming much like those who can't read."

– Reeta Ramamurthy Gupta

ANNEXURES

1. A TRIBUTE TO THE WORK OF STANISLAS DEHAENE
2. A STORY BY STANISLAS DEHAENE
3. A TRIBUTE TO THE WORK OF MARYANNE WOLF
4. THE SCIENCE BEHIND THE HELP MATRIX
5. READING, INDIA AND THE WORLD

ANNEXURE 1

A TRIBUTE TO THE WORK OF STANISLAS DEHAENE

Stanislas Dehaene, a renowned cognitive psychologist and neuroscientist, has made significant contributions to our understanding of the neural mechanisms underlying reading. His thesis, articulated in several seminal works including "Reading in the Brain: The New Science of How We Read," revolves around the idea that reading is not a recent cultural invention but rather a process deeply rooted in the brain's architecture. Dehaene's research delves into the intricate neural circuitry involved in reading, shedding light on how the human brain transforms written symbols into meaningful language.

At the core of Dehaene's thesis is the notion of "neuronal recycling." He proposes that evolution has repurposed pre-existing brain circuits originally developed for other functions, such as object recognition and language processing, to support the uniquely human ability to read. This concept challenges the traditional view that reading is a cultural invention that relies solely on learned skills. Instead, Dehaene argues that the brain's innate capacity for visual recognition and language comprehension provides the foundation upon which reading skills are built.

One key aspect of Dehaene's thesis is the identification of a specialised brain region dedicated to visual word recognition known as the "visual word form area" (VWFA). Through neuroimaging techniques such as functional magnetic resonance imaging (fMRI), Dehaene and his colleagues have demonstrated that the VWFA consistently activates when individuals engage in reading tasks. This finding suggests that the brain has evolved a specialised module for processing written words, further supporting the idea of neuronal recycling in the context of reading.

Furthermore, Dehaene's research has elucidated the role of phonological processing in reading. He proposes that in addition to recognising visual word forms, the brain must also convert these representations into their corresponding sounds – a process known as phonological decoding. This phonological processing, mediated by regions such as the left inferior frontal gyrus and the superior temporal gyrus, is crucial for understanding the pronunciation of written words and is essential for proficient reading.

Another key component of Dehaene's thesis is the importance of literacy acquisition in shaping the organisation of the reading brain. He argues that learning to read induces plastic changes in the brain's neural circuitry, leading to the refinement and specialisation of regions involved in reading. Longitudinal studies have demonstrated that individuals with varying levels of literacy experience corresponding differences in the activation patterns of brain regions involved in reading, further supporting the idea that reading expertise is associated with distinct neural signatures.

Moreover, Dehaene's work extends beyond the realm of basic reading processes to encompass more complex aspects of literacy, such as reading comprehension and dyslexia. By investigating the neural correlates of these phenomena, Dehaene has provided valuable insights into the underlying mechanisms of reading difficulties and potential interventions for individuals with reading disorders.

In summary, Stanislas Dehaene's thesis on reading represents a paradigm shift in our understanding of this fundamental cognitive process. By uncovering the neural mechanisms underlying reading and highlighting the brain's innate capacity for this skill, Dehaene has reshaped the way we conceptualise literacy and its neural basis. His research not only enhances our theoretical understanding of reading but also has important implications for educational practices and interventions aimed at promoting literacy development.

In recent decades, many educational leaders have adopted the scientifically-based Science of Reading model for understanding how students learn to read. The Science of Reading acknowledges the complexity of reading, and presents a pathway for how proficient reading develops. A commonly used metaphor for the complexity of reading, based on the number of skills reading requires, is Scarborough's Reading Rope (see Figure 5). Scarborough (2001) conceptualised lower (word recognition) and upper (language comprehension) strands. All of the skills are intertwined, and as readers become more accurate, fluent, and increasingly automatic through repetition and practice, they become skilled readers.

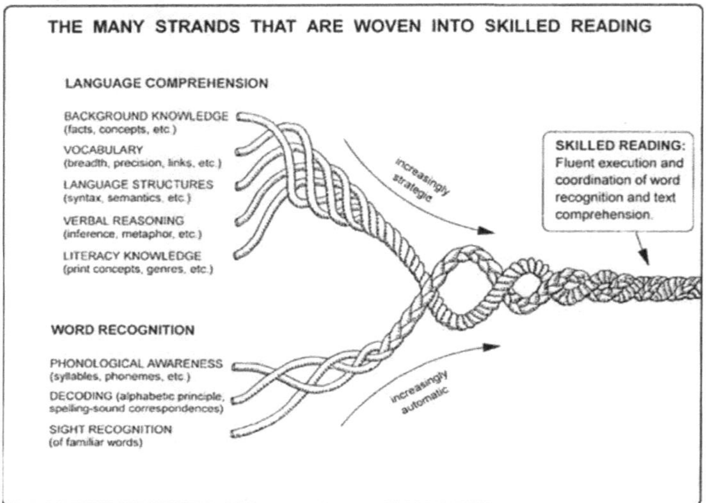

Picture 7 : Scarborough's Reading Rope

Scarborough's Reading Rope

Given the complexity of learning to read, it is important for educators to draw on the decades of reading research that informs the Science of Reading. Specifically, learners require explicit instruction in letter-sound correspondences to acquire reading skills and comprehension (Dehaene, 2010) through letter-by-letter decoding instruction (i.e., phonics instruction; National Reading Panel, 2000). As students learn to decode and automatically recognise words, Ultimately, successful reading is built on a solid foundation in reading skills, such as word recognition and language comprehension, which promote learners' abilities to accurately read words and comprehend the meaning of the text.

ANNEXURE 2D
A STORY BY STANISLAS DEHAENE

The ability to read is not a native feature of the human brain. It has been now proven beyond doubt that we taught ourselves to read.

This understanding was obtained over time and Mr. C had a lot to do with it. Who is Mr. C?

Let me recite a story from 1887. A retired salesperson Mr. C[123] was sitting in an armchair, when he was suddenly not able to read.

The first and most obvious assumption was that there must be something wrong with his eyesight. But Mr. C's ophthalmologist said that his eyes were just fine! The problem was neurological.

So Mr. C went to meet neurologist Dr Joseph Jules who said that the diagnosis could be 'verbal blindness.' Now Mr. C was quite certain that he had lost his mind! How could this be? He could see shapes, objects, people – even numbers! But not letters!! So frustrating!

Mr. C could also write, but with no ability to 'read' what he

123 Paraphrased from 'READING IN THE BRAIN' by Dr Stanislas Dehaene had just written, or if there were errors in what he had written, the continuity of his writing was compromised.

This unique condition that Mr. C found himself in proved one thing – that there is 'specific' neural activity that is needed to recognise letters. Mr. C was not able to do that one basic function which we take for granted – the 'visual recognition of strings of letters!'

Today, neurologists recognise that there is a condition called 'Alexia[124]' which means people cannot recognise strings of letters. It is more of an acquired dyslexia, in the sense that it can show up later in life. In that sense, it is different from dyslexia[125].

In the 21st century, we know for sure that an interface has to be created between the visual system, meaning system and spoken language systems (these light up specific parts of the brain under scan) and show the progression of reading in the brain.

The question therefore remains: if this process is so complex, why did we begin to read? And how is reading connected to our survival as a species.

THINK ABOUT IT!

We were never BORN to read!

If you'd like me to say that in a more complex way, homo sapiens did not possess an innate capacity for reading. Instead, the development of reading skills is the result of millennia

124 The report about Mr. C's 'Alexia' came in 1892.

125 The most common reading disability is dyslexia. It is estimated that 5-10% of the world population is affected by it. Dyslexic people have trouble matching the letters on a page with the sounds they make. Being unable to find the right sound causes the child or adult to spell words incorrectly, have difficulty learning a second language, and have difficulty with reading fluency. It is a genetic disorder.

of cultural evolution, marked by the gradual transition[126] from symbolic communication to complex written language systems.

Whoo!

126 Fig 1.1 has a chronological progression of our evolution from speech to reading

ANNEXURE 3

A TRIBUTE TO THE WORK OF MARYANNE WOLF

Maryanne Wolf is a cognitive neuroscientist and literacy advocate. Wolf's groundbreaking research has illuminated the complex interplay between brain function and reading. Her seminal work, *"Proust and the Squid: The Story and Science of the Reading Brain,"* offers an engaging exploration of how the human brain processes written language. This book is not just a scientific treatise but a celebration of the miraculous evolution of reading and its profound effects on human thought and culture.

Wolf's research delves into the neurological and cognitive mechanisms involved in reading, revealing how our brains have adapted to accommodate this uniquely human skill. By examining how reading shapes our cognition, she has provided invaluable insights into the ways in which literacy influences our intellectual and emotional lives. Her work has underscored the importance of understanding reading not just as a skill but as a complex cognitive process that is crucial to personal and societal development.

In addition to her scientific contributions, Wolf's advocacy for reading is deeply rooted in her belief that literacy is a cornerstone of democracy and intellectual freedom. She has consistently championed the cause of making high-quality reading experiences accessible to all, particularly focusing on the needs of struggling readers and those with learning disabilities.

Her efforts have emphasised that reading is not merely a tool for acquiring information but a vital means of engaging with the world, developing empathy, and fostering critical thinking. Wolf's work has also addressed the impact of digital technology on reading habits. In a time when screens and digital media increasingly dominate our lives, she has raised important questions about how these changes affect our cognitive processes and reading practices. Her concerns about the potential decline in deep, reflective reading due to the prevalence of superficial digital engagement highlight the need for a balanced approach that preserves the depth and richness of traditional reading.

One of Wolf's significant contributions is her advocacy for early literacy education. Her insights into the developmental stages of reading have informed educational practices, including the importance of early intervention and tailored teaching strategies to support all learners. By highlighting the critical periods for reading development and the varying needs of different children, she has helped shape more effective educational frameworks that aim to ensure every child has the opportunity to become a proficient and passionate reader.

Maryanne Wolf's dedication to reading and literacy extends beyond academia. Her public speaking engagements, educational programmes, and collaborations with educators and policymakers have helped bridge the gap between scientific research and practical application. Her ability to communicate complex scientific concepts in accessible and compelling ways has inspired countless individuals to appreciate and nurture the art and science of reading.

Ten years after her first book, having witnessed a changing landscape in modern reading habits, she wrote *Reader, Come Home: The Reading Brain in a Digital World,* which examines how reading on electronic platforms has impacted the brain. Through her research, advocacy, and public engagement, she has not only advanced our knowledge of how reading shapes our brains and our lives but has also worked tirelessly to ensure that the joy and benefits of reading are accessible to all.

Her contributions continue to inspire educators, researchers, and readers alike, reaffirming the transformative power of reading and the enduring importance of nurturing this vital human capability.

ANNEXURE 4D
A SCIENTIFIC EXPLORATION OF THE HELP MATRIX

The HELP matrix is a compelling tool for personal development. Note that there are experts in each of these dimensions and **The Reading Coach** is an expert only on the the power of a sustained reading habit. This chapter is a scientific exploration of the merits of each of the HELP practices, so that you can make an informed choice.

PRACTICE 1: Empathy in inter-personal relationships

Actively practising empathy, the ability to understand and share the feelings of others, plays a crucial role in self-development from both neuroscience and social science perspectives. Empathy involves complex brain networks, primarily the mirror neuron system and the anterior insula. The mirror neurons, located in the premotor cortex, activate when we observe others' emotions, allowing us to 'mirror' their experiences. This

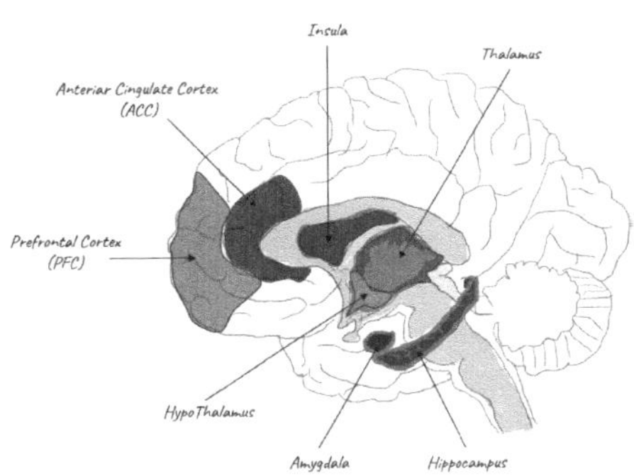

Picture 8 : Parts of the Brain

neural mirroring helps us understand and predict others' behaviours, fostering stronger social connections. The anterior insula is associated with emotional awareness and self-relevance, integrating emotional information and promoting self-regulation. By engaging these neural circuits, empathy enhances our emotional intelligence, helping us manage our own emotions and respond more effectively to social situations. This improved emotional regulation and social understanding contribute significantly to personal growth and resilience.

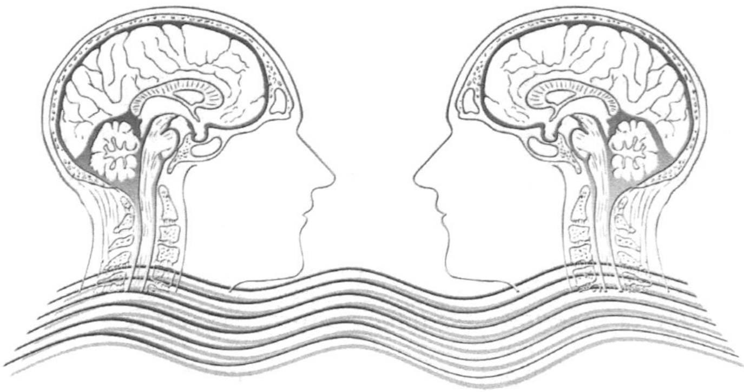

Picture 9 : Artistic Depiction of Empathy

Empathy is fundamental to building and maintaining healthy relationships. It encourages trust, cooperation, and effective communication, all essential for successful interpersonal interactions. Empathetic individuals are more likely to engage in pro-social behaviors, such as offering support and resolving conflicts constructively. This fosters a positive social environment, enhancing both personal and professional relationships. Additionally, empathy aids in perspective-taking, allowing us to appreciate diverse viewpoints and navigate social complexities more adeptly. This capacity to connect with others' experiences broadens our own understanding of the world, leading to increased self-awareness and personal development.

PRACTICE 2: Pushing beyond our comfort zones at work

There is a role we are in and there's a role that we aspire for. The shift from one to the other requires acquiring new skills that will extricate us from our comfort zone. Think about it this way – there's a work group that goes out every Friday night to drink their minds numb. You join a dance class because you're shy and want to be able to express yourself more fluidly.

These choices will have an impact. Whether you join a dance class or a language class or volunteer for an office project after hours, choices shape destiny. If you want to know how your CEO became one, find out what they did as part of their routine over the years when no one was watching!

Stepping out of our comfort zone activates the brain's neuroplasticity, encouraging it to form new neural connections in response to novel challenges. This process engages the prefrontal cortex, which is crucial for decision-making and problem-solving, while stimulating the brain's reward system and releasing dopamine, enhancing motivation and learning. Additionally, facing new experiences reduces reliance on habitual patterns, fostering cognitive flexibility and resilience. This engagement can improve stress management by strengthening the connection between the prefrontal cortex and the amygdala, leading to better emotional regulation, improve overall cognitive agility and enhance personal growth.

From a social science perspective, stepping outside one's comfort zone at work promotes significant personal and professional development. Taking on new roles often requires individuals to develop new skills, adapt to different team dynamics, and navigate unfamiliar responsibilities. This process enhances self-confidence and resilience as individuals learn to manage and overcome challenges. Engaging in diverse roles also broadens one's perspective and understanding

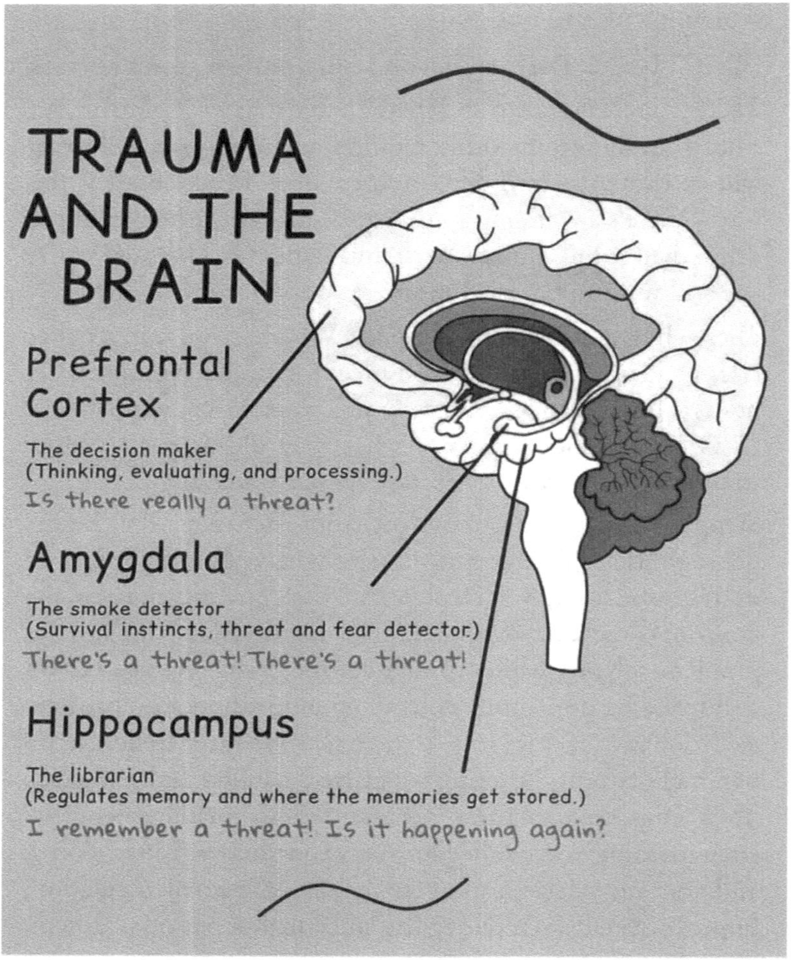

Picture 10 : Trauma and the Brain

This increased awareness and skill set can lead to greater career opportunities and job satisfaction. Furthermore, the experience of working in new roles can improve interpersonal skills, as it often involves interacting with different colleagues and stakeholders, enhancing communication and teamwork abilities.

PRACTICE 3: Reading (this is what the whole book is about!)

PRACTICE 4: TRAVEL

Travel is a great teacher – the very act of leaving home for new pastures opens the mind in a liberating way. Travel too stimulates neuroplasticity, which is the brain's ability to adapt and reorganise itself. Encountering new environments and cultures requires the brain to process novel stimuli, engage in problem-solving, and adapt to unfamiliar situations. This active engagement enhances cognitive flexibility, as the brain's neural networks are challenged and reshaped. For instance, navigating foreign cities or learning new languages can improve memory and spatial awareness, engaging the hippocampus and prefrontal cortex. Furthermore, exposure to different sensory experiences and challenges during travel increases dopamine levels, which are associated with motivation and pleasure, reinforcing positive learning experiences and encouraging continued exploration. The cognitive demands of travel help enhance overall mental agility and resilience.

Travel also broadens one's worldview and improves social skills. Immersing oneself in different cultures fosters empathy and understanding of diverse perspectives, helping to break down cultural barriers and stereotypes. This exposure enhances intercultural competence and improves communication skills, which are vital in an increasingly globalised world. Travel also provides opportunities to develop adaptability and problem-solving skills as individuals navigate new social norms and environments. These experiences promote personal growth by challenging existing beliefs and encouraging self-reflection. Engaging with diverse people and customs can lead to greater self-awareness and a more nuanced understanding of one's own cultural identity and values.

Travel teaches us new things about ourselves and converts us into veritable raconteurs! Travel provides us with a wealth of stories to share with people, whether friends and family and you can become a conversationalist, sharing tales of where you have been and what you have seen.

PRACTICE 5: Committed pursuit of any discipline

A committed pursuit of disciplines such as cooking, gardening, or painting significantly contributes to self-development from both neuroscience and social science perspectives. And before we make the cardinal mistake of looking down on people who are not in the race to work for money, we must thank every homemaker in the world for their commitment to raising happy families. And they're living example of being extremely mature and intelligent, while not necessarily being readers.

Engaging in a dedicated practice enhances cognitive and emotional functioning. When individuals commit to a discipline, they actively participate in learning, problem-solving, and creative processes, all of which stimulate brain plasticity. For instance, mastering cooking or painting involves acquiring new skills, which activates brain regions like the hippocampus, responsible for learning and memory, and the prefrontal cortex, involved in planning and decision-making. Regular practice in any discipline can lead to structural changes in the brain, such as increased grey matter density, which supports improved cognitive abilities and emotional regulation. Additionally, the focused attention required in these activities can enhance executive function and attention span, while the satisfaction and sense of achievement from progress can boost levels of dopamine, reinforcing motivation and pleasure.

Pursuing a discipline also fosters personal growth and social benefits. Commitment to activities like cooking or painting often involves setting and achieving goals, which builds self-discipline and confidence. These activities can also enhance emotional well-being by providing a creative outlet for self-expression and stress relief. Furthermore, participating in community groups or classes related to these disciplines promotes social interaction, fostering a sense of belonging and social support. This engagement helps individuals develop interpersonal skills, empathy, and a stronger sense of community. The shared experiences and learning processes inherent in such pursuits can lead to greater self-awareness and improved relational dynamics.

The ardent pursuit of any discipline stimulates cognitive and emotional growth by engaging neural circuits involved in learning and creativity, while also enhancing social skills and personal well-being.

PRACTICE 6: Spiritual immersion

Spiritual immersion is one of the cornerstones of self-development. Meditation and breath-focused techniques have been shown to alter brain structure and function positively. Regular meditation increases gray matter density in the hippocampus, which is associated with memory and emotional regulation, and the prefrontal cortex, which governs executive functions and self-control. These changes enhance cognitive flexibility, emotional stability, and stress resilience. Additionally, mindfulness meditation reduces activity in the amygdala, a brain region involved in stress responses, promoting a calmer, more balanced emotional state. Journalling, particularly reflective or expressive writing, has been linked to reduced symptoms of anxiety and depression, partly due to its effects on the brain's stress-processing areas and its ability to improve emotional processing and self-awareness.

Meditation fosters significant personal growth by enhancing self-awareness and emotional intelligence. Journalling, for instance, allows individuals to process and reflect on their experiences, leading to greater insight into their thoughts, emotions, and behaviours. This self-reflection promotes emotional regulation and personal clarity, which are crucial for effective interpersonal relationships and decision-making. Meditation and breath-focused practices contribute to improved focus, reduced stress, and increased empathy, all of which enhance social interactions and personal well-being. These practices also encourage a more mindful approach to daily life, helping individuals respond to challenges with greater calm and resilience.

ANNEXURE 5D

READING, INDIA AND THE WORLD

Reading didn't really begin with 'books.' A book[127] is 'a set of printed sheets of paper that are held together inside a cover; a long written work.' This definition rules out clay tablets, papyrus, scrolls and similar…even diagrams drawn on walls of caves and temples. The latter is how reading began.

Reading was a step up from listening, which is how our journey to transmit information began. One of the oldest oral traditions is believed to be the legend of the volcano called Budj Bim, told 37,000 years ago by the aboriginal Gunditjmara people of Australia! There is also the story of a bird hunt passed down generations by the aboriginal Tjapwurung people – again in Australia – estimated to be between 5,000 to 10,000 years old. In India, the date of oral composition of the Rig Veda may date as far back as 6000–4000 BC based on Bal Gangadhar Tilak's astronomical research into the position of the constellation Orion[128]. Other scholars, however, say the oral composition was around 1500 to 1000 BC; but it was written down much later.

Along the way came the written traditions developed around

127 Merriam Webster
128 He wrote this in his book, *Orion: Or Researches Into The Antiquity Of The Vedas* (1893)

3200 BC by Sumerian scribes in the ancient city-state of Uruk, in present-day Iraq, as a means of recording transactions. This cuneiform writing (grooves in clay tablets) survived 3,000[129] years, during which the "Epic of Gilgamesh," ancient Sumerian[130] poems and stories written on clay tablets in the Akkadian[131] language around 1800 BC, emerged.

The Egyptian text, *The Teaching of Ptahhatp,* is also believed to be written around 2300 BC.

The Rig Veda was also written down around this time and the other vedas are estimated to have been written around 600 BC. There was also a multi-page book dating to about 660 BC, the Etruscan Gold Book. Alphabetical writing came up only in the 1st century AD.

We are faced with too many unanswered questions and several writings that have either disappeared or not been accessed yet!

- Indian trade to modern day Syria existed as early as the 7th millennium BC. How did they keep accounts?

- What happened to all the manuscripts destroyed at Takshashila? How old were they and where were they sourced from? (The university was up in 5th century BC and destroyed in the 5th century AD)

- What happened to the millions of books destroyed at Nalanda? (Set up in 5th century AD and destroyed in the 12th century AD)

- The Harappan civilisation lasted from 3300 BC to 1300 BC and they had 270 characters. An ink-pot was discovered in

129 The first printing technique - multiple copies of symbols or glyphs with a master type punch made of hard metal- was also first developed around 3000 BC in ancient Sumer
130 Of ancient Babylonia (south of Baghdad) in Iraq.
131 Akkad is the ancient region in what is now central Iraq.

the excavations. Where are the Harappan writings?

How sure are we about all these dates and timelines, if we acknowledge all the disappeared books?

The books that survived are those that were copied again and again down generations. The ones that were copied down were considered useful; for example, the Rig Veda which is still in 'active use.'

Print came later. The first printed book used Chinese woodblock print technology – the Diamond Sutra in 868 AD. The Koreans had their own methods too but these books were expensive and rare. However, literacy started growing after 1100 AD. Later, Gutenberg made printing mass and accessible, followed by successive improvements in technology, making a book available in every hand today.

ADDITIONAL READING

This book is a scientific work. We presume nothing but consider everything. Even though we have given several references in the footnotes, to understand specific ideas better, please read the following additional written resources.

1. Lucien Febvre, Henri-Jean Martin, translated by David Gerard (1958),'The Coming of the Book: The Impact of Printing 1450-1800,'New Left Books.

2. Simpson, W. (1971), 'The Ancient Near East', New York, Harcourt Brace Jovanovich (HPJ publishers).

3. Walter J. Ong (1982), 'Orality and Literacy: The Technologizing of the Word,' Routledge.

4. Alberto Manguel (1997), 'A History Of Reading', Penguin.

5. Morgan, TJ (1998), 'Literate Education in the Hellenistic and Roman Worlds', Cambridge University Press.

6. National Reading Panel (U.S.) & National Institute of Child Health and Human Development (U.S.) (2000). 'Report of the National Reading Panel (Teaching children to read): an evidence-based assessment of the scientific research literature on reading and its implications for reading instruction', U.S.

Dept. of Health and Human Services.

7. Nicolas Basbanes (2005) 'Every Book Its Reader: The Power of the Printed Word to Stir the World', Harper Perennial.

8. Thomas Suddendorf, Michael C. Corballis (2007), 'The evolution of foresight: What is mental time travel, and is it unique to humans?', Cambridge University Press

9. Ed(s Simon Eliot, Jonathan Rose (2007), 'Companion to the History of the Book', Wiley-Blackwell.

10. Dessales, J.L. (2009), 'Why we talk: The evolutionary origins of language,' Oxford University Press, Oxford.

11. Olson, David R.; Torrance, Nancy (February 16, 2009), 'The Cambridge Handbook of Literacy', Cambridge University Press.

12. Cross, Andrew (2009), 'The Development of the Greek Alphabet within the Chronology of the ANE', University of Calgary.

13. Charles W.J. Withers, translated by Miles Ogborn (2010), Geographies of the Book, Routledge.

14. Dehaene, Stanislas, Felipe Pegado, Lucia W Braga, Paulo Ventura, Gilberto Nunes Filho, Antoinette Jobert, Ghislaine Dehaene-Lambertz, Régine Kolinsky, José Morais, Laurent Cohen (2010),'How learning to read changes the cortical networks for vision and language', SCIENCE, Vol 330, Issue 6009.

15. Colin Barras (2010), 'Is an Aboriginal tale of an ancient volcano the oldest story ever told?', science.org.

16. Woods, Christopher (2010), 'The earliest Mesopotamian writing', Oriental Institute Museum Publications.

17. Wayman, Erin (2012), 'Becoming Human: The Evolution of Walking Upright', Smithsonian Magazine.

18. Jorge Carrión, Translated by Peter Bush (2013) 'Bookshops-A Reader's History', Biblioasis.

19. Uomini, Natalie Thaïs, Georg Friedrich Meyer (2013), 'Shared Brain Lateralization Patterns in Language and Acheulean Stone Tool Production: A Functional Transcranial Doppler Ultrasound Study.'

20. Roderick Cave, Sara Ayad (2014) 'The History of the Book in 100 Books: The Complete Story, From Egypt to E-Book', Firefly Books.

21. 4. Gruss, L.T. & Scmitt, D.(2015), 'Evolution of the human pelvis: changing adaptations to bipedalism, obstetrics and thermoregulation', Philosophical Transactions of the Royal Society.

22. Elder, Gregory (2017), 'In ancient Egypt, scribal school was the path to the priesthood and the good life,' Redlands Daily Facts.

23. Mark Seidenberg (2017), 'Language at the Speed of Sight', Basic Books.

24. G. Kylene Beers, Robert E. Probst (2017), 'Disrupting Thinking: Why How We Read Matters', Scholastic.

25. Scott, John C (2018), 'The Phoenicians and the Formation of the Western World',Comparative Civilizations Review.

26. Martin Lyons, (2022), 'The History of Illiteracy in the Modern World Since 1750', Palgrave Macmillan.

27. Irene Vallejo (2022) 'Papyrus: The Invention of Books in the Ancient World', Alfred A Knopf.

28. Max S Bennett (2024), 'A Brief History Of Intelligence', William Collins.

29. A L Basham(2022), 'The Wonder That Was India', Pan Macmillan India.

30. Joshua Hammer (2025), 'The Mystery of the World's Oldest Writing System Remained Unsolved Until Four Competitive Scholars Raced to Decipher It,' Smithsonian Magazine.